ON PAST TEAMMATES

"Randy Myers was the real psycho of the club. Here's a guy who goes to the mound with a knife in his pocket. You'd ask him, 'Well, Randy, what's the knife for?' He'd go, 'See, you never know what might happen. If a guy charges me, I'll slice his throat.' You wonder about a guy like that."

"Keith Hernandez and I had our differences. I guess that's well known by now. But if we disagreed, we made up not long afterward. That ought to be well known, too, but it isn't."

ON OPPOSING PLAYERS

"I've batted against Rick Reuschel often. Some fans look at him and think he's pitching from a chair. You look at him and you think he's got nothing going for him. He's overweight and slow, or so you think. That's how he gets you. Because he's smart and he's mastered the way he pitches."

ON THE PRESS

"I've heard for years that the New York press is the worst in the country. In other cities, the press wants to build you up if you've got talent. In New York, they want to tear you down. I've fought for my own survival in New York, just to keep my head above water."

ON DARRYL STRAWBERRY

"I'm the type of person who doesn't dislike anybody. I don't like to go around saying negative things. When I say things that may hurt someone, I do it because it's the truth."

HARD LEARNIN'
Darryl Strawberry

with Don Gold

B

BERKLEY BOOKS, NEW YORK

The statistics starting on p. 251 and
all material about Darryl Strawberry contained
in the New York Mets Press Information Guide 1989
are used with the kind permission of the New
York Mets, Jay Horwitz, Director of Public Relations.

HARD LEARNIN'

A Berkley Book / published by arrangement with
Strawberry Pro Sports, Inc. (f/s/o Darryl Strawberry)

PRINTING HISTORY
Berkley edition / October 1990

ISBN 0-425-12651-X

PRINTED IN THE UNITED STATES OF AMERICA

10 9 8 7 6 5 4 3 2 1

HARD LEARNIN'

1

Early Days

I can't remember a time when I didn't love the game of baseball. When I was a little kid, it was the major distraction in my life. While other kids in our south Los Angeles neighborhood were moving down the path to trouble, some of it dangerous trouble, I was the one who grabbed his glove and headed for the field.

Baseball gave me goals to achieve, to strive for; it provided a purpose for my life. It helped me deal with my frustrations and it gave me joy.

That's how it's always been for me.

Today I'm in the major leagues, and you can't do better than that.

Sometimes I thank God that I was lucky enough and talented enough to make it. Others in my neighborhood didn't. For those of us who had athletic skills, growing up meant going to school, getting an education, trying to be successful. For the others, it was gang violence, drugs, a lot of bad stuff. Those of us who lived there had a choice, good or bad—you had to make the decision.

The neighborhood itself didn't look like a ghetto; maybe a "ghetto" is a state of mind. I'd call the house I grew up in a decent house.

I lived with my father and my mother and my two brothers and two sisters. We were a popular family in the neighborhood. We were respected; we were good kids. My brothers and I were into athletics; everybody knew that about us. My sisters were sweethearts—they would take care of little kids from other families if the parents had to go to work or were away.

We all knew that the other side existed, of course, but I was never tempted by it. I'm not easy to intimidate now and I wasn't easy to intimidate as a kid. Most of the guys I hung out with were athletic. We had teams; we'd play football, basketball, and baseball against teams from other neighborhoods.

I always knew one of the main rules: when the game ended, I had to prepare for school the next day. There was no fooling around about that in my family. That was my mother Ruby's way. And she was in charge. When our games were over, if some of the other guys decided to do things that I didn't think were right, I'd just go in another direction. I wasn't the kind of kid who wanted to fight, to steal, to hang around and get drunk or stoned. I had other plans.

The others guys always talked about that. They admired me, and some of them even told me so. I had a goal from the first time I knew I could play ball: I wanted to be a pro baseball player someday. I used to tell the other guys that. "I don't have time for all this *stuff*," I'd say. "I'm looking in another direction, one that's going to lead me to greatness."

I was 13 when I first believed that for sure. Before that, I was just a kid who played a lot of sports. When I got to junior high, though, sports became my dream, a way to greatness.

My mother, Ruby, always supported me; she was behind all of her kids, in fact. She was the chief. There wasn't any late night hanging out for her kids. No way. There was a certain time that we had to be at home at night. Of course, some of us—mostly my brother Ronnie and I—would wait until she went to sleep and then sneak out the window and hang out with our friends.

If she caught you, watch out! You'd be in trouble, no doubt about it. But it wasn't a serious temper. She didn't get upset about minor things. She wanted to raise her kids to be decent kids, to be respected, not to grow up to be wild animals. She taught us to realize that life is what you make it. Don't take bad chances. Do things to make your family proud. Try to achieve something. My brothers, my sisters, and I grew up learning that. We grew up with the respect of our neighbors, and even today, as adults out there in the world, we conduct ourselves the way our mother wanted us to.

Achievement is something that is developed inside of you when you're growing up. Inside your mind. Running through your bloodstream. We all learned that: Michael, the oldest; Ronnie; and our two sisters, Regina and Michelle.

Today, we've given Ruby eleven grandchildren, and she's as good at being a grandmother as she was being our mother.

Ruby taught each of us to be someone, to be successful in life. She didn't want her kids out in the streets getting into trouble.

I never did develop an interest in hurting others. Sure, if something happened to my mother, my sisters, my brothers, my own kids, I'd probably stop being a low-keyed person. But otherwise, no. That's not what I was taught.

I know that the other side exists. I grew up with some kids who turned out to be terrible guys.

There's that old saying, "There but for the grace of god..." Well I think that the rules of our house, the rules Ruby set for us, kept me from that kind of fate.

But there's more to it than that. My mother wasn't a selfish person. She cared about her kids and wanted them to grow up happy. When you're selfish and you think about yourself and the things you want most of the time, you don't think about what's surrounding you. That makes a big difference. You've got to think about others. You've got to have feelings for them.

People who think only about themselves get into trouble. When you think about yourself, you look at things and you say, "Wow, I want that" or "I want to be like that." Sometimes a choice that seems easy to make from that point of view is the wrong choice.

That's something that I learned just by living with Ruby.

And living with my father, too, at least until I was 13, when he left.

Today, I'm a motivated baseball player. Sometimes, I wonder where I got that attitude. I've been asked whether there was an athlete I watched when I was a kid, an athlete who was an example to me.

Some people may find it a little strange, but when I was growing up, as a little kid, I really didn't have any heroes in baseball. I probably didn't go to Dodger Stadium more than three times. Of course, I knew about the L.A. Lakers and I liked the way Jerry West played. You know, Mr. Clutch. He was the guy you could depend upon; you could pass the ball to him in crucial situations and he'd be calm and put it in the bucket. When I got older and really got into baseball, my hero was Pete Rose. I just loved his style of baseball, the way he played the game head-first, flying. He was a hard-nosed player and I admired that.

But who I really watched was my father. He was very athletic. We used to watch him play baseball. He was a great player. He played for a team at the post office in Los Angeles, where he worked. He was a pitcher. I mean he could really pitch. He'd throw extremely hard, and he was fast and could hit too—he could hit the ball a *long* way.

I think he had the opportunity to play professional ball, but he got hurt and never made it past semi-pro ball. He was an extremely good athlete. I saw him play football, too. What's interesting is that my size is like my father's size; if you look at my brothers and sisters, they're smaller, like my mother. But I've got my father's build, and he was strong.

When I was growing up, though, it was difficult living with him. He didn't take the time to spend with us, with his family. He had five kids; he had a commitment, a responsibility he didn't live up to. Maybe it frustrated him. Maybe he wanted to do things that he couldn't do because he had a house full of people to worry about. If you're going to make a home, you make a home and take care of it. If you don't, you're going to suffer the consequences.

When I was a kid, I really didn't understand all that. It was hard for me because my father wouldn't take the time to sit and talk to me about what was right and what wasn't. Instead of talking to me about staying out of trouble in school, he'd just give me a whupping. For him, that was the answer. But that isn't the key to making kids behave, to inspiring them to be successful. Taking out a belt doesn't replace the kind of love you need from a father.

He never sat down with me and said, "Well, you're growing up now, and you have to start making decisions." That was up to my mother to do.

My father was a gambler and that's an addiction. We weren't really aware of it as kids until one night, when things weren't going well, and he came home after he had been drinking a lot. He was loud, shouting and fussing at our mother. We all woke up.

We came out to see what was going on. We were all sitting at the table, listening to him, and then we just couldn't take any more. We were young—thirteen, fourteen, fifteen. My brother Michael just told him to get out of there and leave us alone.

My father acted like he was going to hurt Michael. So me and Ronnie got serious about it. We weren't going to let him hurt our brother. It got nasty.

Things did calm down, finally. He left, but it was a terrible night.

He came back a day or two later, and that's when Ruby told him that she couldn't take it any more; she wanted a divorce.

As far as I was concerned, he left my life at that time. All of us were disturbed by what had happened. But there was some relief that he had gone.

I didn't talk to him for years. When I was in high school, he came around from time to time, but I didn't have much to say to him. I guess it was a hurting feeling on my part. Maybe I should have been more of a man, taken a step toward him. But it was hard for me. I was just in high school, and I didn't know how to respond to my father after I'd been hurt.

What was sad was that he knew who his son was. I mean, there was so much talk about me when I was in high school, because I was a great basketball player and I was being called the best high school baseball player in the country. I guess he had heard all that and wanted to come around and see what was going on in my life. So he just started showing up at a lot of my games. We would talk, but not much. And a lot of scouts would talk to him when they found out he was my father. They wanted to find out from him how I felt about playing pro ball. The truth was that Ruby was in control of that. But she was working all day, at the phone company.

We never talked about Dad. And he never apologized. He didn't have to. You can see guilt all over a person's face. Years later, I realized that I was a man and he was a man. Now, I do talk to him. I want to buy him a nice house and a car, whatever he needs. I hold no regrets. I can't be like that. And that's partly because of my mother. She told me that I had no reason to feel sorry for my father and no reason, anymore, to hold anything against him. That's how she feels.

She's truly wonderful. All those years without him, she went about what she had to do. She worked and took care of us. It's amazing when I look back on it today.

Fortunately, we weren't the kind of kids who asked for everything. We lived with what we had and we went about our business, went to school, got our educations and learned to believe in ourselves.

We believed in getting an education, but we also believed in being happy. What made me happiest in high school was playing sports. I approached sports very seriously then. Like I do now. I was determined to do well, and nothing would stop me. I was a self-motivator. It was inside of me.

Everybody used to say, Straw's a great athlete; he plays football; he plays baseball; he plays basketball. But what made me feel best was that they saw me as a truly good, honest, clean person.

What's funny is that my mother really didn't know much about sports. She finally saw me play one day when I was a senior in high school. It was the first time she ever came to see me play basketball, and it was in the playoffs.

My sisters told me that she was thrilled to see me on the floor. "I couldn't believe it," she told them. "That was my son running up and down the court like that. He had so much energy, playing the way he was playing."

She realized then what it was like to play hard, that I had to go through a lot of hard practice to play like that. She realized, too, why I would come home and lay around, just do my homework and go to sleep.

Of course, I didn't choose to go on in basketball. I chose baseball. I did it because I thought it was a very special game.

It's a pattern between you and the pitcher. It's not so difficult playing basketball, putting the ball in the bucket. For a lot of guys, shooting comes naturally. But it takes a different mentality to play baseball.

I think you have to be smarter to play baseball. There's a lot more thinking involved in what you have to do on the baseball field as opposed to the basketball court. In baseball, you have to remember so much; you have to know how to be a defensive player; you have to know what it's like to face the top pitchers in the game. It's you against the guy on the mound. That's it. Sure, in basketball you have the greats: Magic Johnson, Larry Bird, Michael Jordan. But those guys run up and down the court, and, not taking anything

13

away from them, running up and down the court is not too complicated.

In the NBA, if you're really good, you score half the time. In baseball, it's more difficult—three out of ten is great. When you're facing some of the top pitchers in the business, it's extremely challenging. It's not like shooting an easy basket or catching a pass. That's a hard pitch that may come at you, and you've got to react quickly.

It's a challenge and that's why I chose it as my sport. I knew when I was a kid that it was going to be a tough game to master. But I felt in my mind that I would achieve a lot in the game, that baseball would make me more aware of the world.

If you really look at this game, you can see the tension around it. Fans pay attention to everything you do. Basketball is a team effort, but in baseball, you become known as a star and you're supposed to do this or that every day. In basketball, if you lose, the team loses. In baseball, if you don't produce on a given night, you made the mistake, you lost the game. You're fingered.

It took me a while to learn that, that challenge. It brings out the best in players, I think. It inspires you. I look at Gary Carter and I respect how dedicated he is to his work. He's very intense on the field, totally dedicated to his profession. Gary wants to achieve a lot. I can understand that and I can relate to it. I look at myself and I say, man, I really want to do well. I really don't care too much what anybody else is going to think about me—they can call me a hot dog or whatever, but I want to do things that nobody who plays the same position can do. If God gave me the talent to achieve, why not take advantage of it?

I've really thought about the whole idea of being blessed. There are a lot of good athletes in professional baseball. When you're one of the special ones, it's because of a blessing the Lord put on you. He put me in my situation for a reason, an example, to show people that you can be as great as you want to be. At the same time, you're still the same person you always were, nothing has changed in your character. That's the way I was raised. To take it all in stride.

When you get too tied up in what you do, whatever it is, you can start thinking you're better than the next person.

"What are you coming over here for, wanting to talk to me. Don't you know who I am?" That sort of thing. Some people get to that point, and it's a disgrace.

It's a bad example for the younger generation, who see you as a role model. An athlete is no better than the next person. We all have to do the same things to live together on this planet—we have to eat and sleep and thank the Lord for letting us be here the next day. We have to brush our teeth and comb our hair and tie our shoes the same way.

I know that I'm being watched by kids all over the country, and what I do influences them. I think that's why I get a lot of good responses from parents. They tell me how much their kids admire me, and they thank me for being such a great role model. They know what I've been through, playing in New York and dealing with the press. I always bounce back from controversy, though, regroup and come out and continue to do what I have to do.

Sometimes I say things out of frustration; a lot of people understand that, though, they understand me. They see how much pressure I have. Baseball built me up, and the press tries to tear me down, writes negative things about me. But my fans understand. They know that I always seem to come out and finish the season with talent and energy. Parents tell their kids that it's wonderful to idolize someone who has his head on right, a guy who speaks his mind and doesn't hide anything. They can say that about me.

I have nothing to hide. I think that's what

a lot of parents know when they come to me and tell me that their kids admire me. The parents tell me that they appreciate what I've done for their kids. "My kid has changed so much just by following your career and knowing the type of person you are," they tell me.

And when I'm around those people, my fans, I'm an open person. I'm not one of those guys who goes away, who doesn't have time for the fans. You know, "Sorry, I've got other things to do." What more can you do than sit there and shake a kid's hand, sign an autograph? It might be a big lift in his life, and that's a reward in itself.

If you're one of the top players, one of the popular players, you know that fans really enjoy getting your autograph. They want it and it's nothing that they kid around about. That's flattering. They're telling you that they're thrilled by the way you perform on the field and the way you carry yourself. I always feel good about giving autographs. It's part of my job. It's a great feeling to know that people appreciate you and know who you are.

I get tons of fan mail. Some of it I save and have shipped down to spring training. There's time to spare down there, and I can sit and send postcards to those who've written to me. I get a lot of encouraging letters. Kids saying how much they love me, that they don't ever want me to leave the Mets. Stuff like that. It's nice to know that kids think of you that way; some of them are just seven or eight years old.

Of course, it's sometimes difficult for me to have a quiet meal in a restaurant. Someone usually recognizes me and wants to talk. Sure, that can be a bother. But I tell myself not to fret about it. It tickles me, in fact, when someone comes up to tell me that they've seen my daughter's pictures in the paper and how cute she is. Or my son, Darryl Jr. People come up and ask me about him because they've seen him with me on television when we've gone to a basketball game at the Garden. People will see him and love him. I'll get letters from young girls offering to be his babysitter.

I'm grateful for all of that. I try not to complain about the attention I get just by being good at what I do for a living. I know that part of my success depends on the following of those who appreciate what I do and how well I do it.

There's more to it than that, though—I'm a religious person. That's important, too.

I know that I have to be grateful for all the great things that have happened in my life. I don't sit around and take those things for granted. I never feel that, well, this is how it's supposed to be for me. I feel it's this way because the Man upstairs made it this way. He put me here for a particular reason, to set an example. To show parents and kids that you can be successful, but you can always be yourself as well. You never have to change. That's the message I want to be able to deliver to people.

I learned that from my mother. She believes, too. She could sit right down next to someone and say that her son hasn't changed at all. She'll say he's probably as stubborn as ever, but there's one thing about him and that's he hasn't changed. People who knew me when I was growing up say it, too.

The truth is I never learned what the reasons are for changing. Why change? What does that prove? Why put up a front, just to be more fashionable? Why be someone you're not?

Yes, I have noticed players change. But what do they get out of it?

To me, I'm the one who matters. I've got to know who I am all the time. I don't want to worship any false idols.

I've been known to give advice, of course, to others, but mostly family, not teammates. If there's a family problem, I want to be there, because my family has always been there for me. The family is where my love and support come from. If anything serious happens, I want to be involved in it.

But I've learned that it's a big mistake to get involved with your teammates on that level. If you decide you want to speak up on a teammate's situation, you run a big risk— they might think you're trying to be a damper on what they've done, feel you're busting into their business, which is none of yours.

Drugs, for example. Sometimes you know about other people; sometimes you don't know. When guys who are professionals live together for six months a year, they hide their problems. It could be that the problem is the only thing they're doing that they don't want anybody else to know about. It's a matter of pride. They don't want anyone to know what's going on. What's crazy about that is that people find out if so-and-so is doing drugs. Not because a teammate knows or tells, but because the guy with the problem is more open about it with the people on the outside than he is with his own teammates. Your so-called friends on the outside, are the ones who tend to leak the dirty secrets.

That's part of the learning process. And learning is something I've been into ever since I first picked up a bat when I was a kid. It's just that it gets more complicated the older you get. When I was young, it wasn't so difficult. And my teacher had plenty to offer.

Before I got to high school, I met John Moseley. He was an assistant coach at Compton College and he was a neighbor of ours. He had a job—he was a truck driver—but he spent a lot of his spare time with the Strawberry brothers. His dream was to make all of us into major league players. I was playing on a kids team called the Black Sox. He saw me play, and he knew that Michael and Ronnie had talent, too. So he set out to help all of us.

John's a short guy, maybe five-seven, and husky. Very smart. He was the one guy who taught me the most about baseball. I think he had played back in the negro league.

He had been working with Michael and Ronnie when I dropped by. John told a writer (William Nack, in *Sports Illustrated*) that when he talked to Mike and Ronnie, I was the one who listened and absorbed.

He was right about that.

"Darryl was never a guy to mess around with girls," he told Nack. "Baseball is all Darryl talked about. He was a baseball fanatic." He was right about that, too.

There was a park not far from where we lived, and John took us there all the time.

He stressed the fundamentals, over and over again. He'd hit fly balls all afternoon. We'd work hard with him, and then he'd be like a father and take us out for some food.

He would lecture us, as well, about doing well in school and staying away from the meanness of the streets.

I had natural ability; I knew that, but I needed the insight John had to offer, and I was grateful to get it. He made me sharper. At age 14 I was hitting balls to the next diamond, but I still had a lot to learn. I was playing with the older guys in the neighborhood, guys up to 18 years old. I was tall and thin, and John liked the way I played. He saw the potential in me.

He used to tell everybody who would listen, "I've got the best kid of all. He's going to be in the major leagues and he's going to dominate."

He taught me how to run the bases. He taught me how to hit the cutoff man. He taught me how to play the outfield.

He taught me how to go back on balls, the ones you tend to misjudge when you're a kid. He taught me about hitting. He made me focus on how to pick up a ball from the pitcher's hand, instead of just watching the pitcher's motion and being distracted by it.

He used to tell me, over and over, "You're

being distracted by the pitcher's motion." Years later, when I was watching Fernando Valenzuela pitch to someone else, I realized how important that advice was to me. Fernando's motion was a show in itself; it was easy to pay attention to it and forget about the ball in his hand.

Once I learned the lessons that John was teaching me, everything seemed to be easier.

I guess it would be easy to say that John was my father during that period in my life, after my father had left our house. And there's some truth to that. He was like a father to all of the Strawberry boys. I remember that I would hate to get up and go work out, but John would come over to get me up and to the park.

"He's asleep," one of my sisters would tell John.

"Well, go in there and wake him up," John would order. "I'll sit right here on the porch for him until he gets dressed. He's going to work out."

He was right. I got up and went out with him.

He taught all of us more than how to play baseball. He taught us moral lessons, too. He knew we came from a good background, that we'd been raised by Ruby, but he wanted to make sure that we stayed that way.

After John, there was Brooks Hurst. I went to Crenshaw High School in Los Angeles, and Brooks was the baseball coach. My brother Michael had told Brooks about me; Michael was the team's center fielder when I got to Crenshaw. At the time I guess I was troubled by my father's leaving us. I was at that age when I was moody; I had an attitude.

I had my ups and downs with Brooks. I wanted to play every day and he wanted me to pitch. There was another guy playing right field for the Crenshaw team, and he was having a good year, so Brooks stuck with him. But I felt that I should have been playing in right field; I've always been a right fielder. I did play a bit of first base and I did pitch a little bit, as both starter and reliever. But I didn't like to pitch. Too much wear and tear on my arm.

At one point, I came in after an inning and Brooks didn't think I was coming in fast enough. He told me that I'd have to hustle. I guess I trotted in instead of running in. We lost the game. Afterward, Brooks was getting on quite a few people.

He grabbed me on my uniform and started pulling me, telling me, "You're just out of tenth grade and you think you're a superstar already."

I was pissed off at that point. I took my

uniform off and said, "Man, I don't even want to play anymore." I left.

I was gone for the rest of that season. Then Brooks and I talked about it, a good talk. I realized how much I loved baseball. There was no way I could hide from that. I wanted to play and Crenshaw had a great team. So I talked to Brooks and told him I'd changed over the summer and that I had settled down and gotten myself together. I wanted to come back and play.

He agreed to let me come back.

When I think about that time, I realize what a super guy Brooks was. A big guy, tall, lanky, he was in his thirties. He was a good coach; he stressed fundamentals, the way John Moseley had. He worked us hard, but he believed in having fun, too.

And Brooks was white, not black, coaching a team of black players. He had the greatest black players in the city—the best team in the city during my junior year.

Chris Brown was on the team; he's in the majors, too, now. It was a team that was just unbelievable for a high school team. Even the scouts had never seen a high school team like that one.

They called us the lumber company, like the Pittsburgh Pirates. We had mashers all up and down the lineup. The scouts thought

I was a senior, I was playing so strong. They'd ask Brooks about the kid Strawberry, the senior. Brooks would have to tell them, no, he's a junior. They'd say, you've got a kid who's a junior and he's hitting like that?

Brooks got a lot of pleasure out of that team. Coaching was his life; he loved it. But guess what? We played for the city championship and lost to Granada Hills. John Elway pitched against us. I wish he had stayed with football back then. He did more than pitch; he pitched and played third base. It was the final game for the championship, in Dodger Stadium. Elway started at third, then came in to relieve. I started in right field, then relieved.

It was some game, even if we did lose.

I still keep in touch with John Moseley and Brooks today. Every time I go out to California, I find John. Before spring training, I go out there to get into shape. He'll come out to the park and watch me work out. He still lives around there, the way he did when he took the Strawberry brothers out for instruction.

When I'm out there, I try to stop by to see Brooks, to say hello, see how he's doing. I don't forget.

He had a great program at Crenshaw, a very intelligent guy running a very smooth program. He brought a lot of recognition to the school. When I left there, I was ready for professional baseball.

John and Brooks saw the qualities in me that I respected in others. I had a lot of pride about my ability. I hated to lose. And I wanted to improve, to learn how to be a better player.

So when the baseball draft took place in June 1980, I was happy and proud to be the first choice, taken by the Mets. My brother Michael had joined the Dodgers' farm system that same year, but he didn't last past 1981. I was the Strawberry to carry the family banner, it seemed.

The free-agent draft means tension and reward for those high school players involved in it. I remember that a lot of eager agents were calling Ruby, pleading for the right to represent me. Some of them called me and I just referred them to her. If I couldn't trust her, who could I trust?

Money offers fell on the table. "They wanted to tell him about the big money," Ruby told a *New York Times* reporter. "They feel that kids brought up in the ghetto— money excites them."

We did pick an agent, Richman Bry, and days later I got the first large sum I'd ever seen. The signing bonus was $200,000, the largest signing bonus the Mets had ever offered.

I told my mother, "All I want is a car, Mom, and you take the rest." I got the Buick Riviera I wanted, and my mother got the car she'd always wanted, a Datsun 280Z.

What's funny, looking back on those days, is that I never really thought a lot about what was going on in the draft, the money, my future—all of it. I always figured that if I didn't play baseball, I'd go on to college on a basketball scholarship. I remember thinking that it would be great to be in college playing two sports.

When the Mets put their money down, I looked over the entire situation and told the Mets that I wanted to get to the major league level by a certain time. If I couldn't be assured of that, it didn't do me any good to sign a pro contract. They guaranteed me that I'd be in the major leagues within two and a half years. One of the Met executives told me, "There's no way you're not going to be in the major leagues. You've got such unbelievable talent that you'll have to be up soon. If you develop like we think you will during the course of your minor league career, you'll be at the major league level before you know it."

Of course, if I hadn't signed with the Mets, I couldn't have signed with anyone else.

That's the rule. I would have gone on to school instead, played ball at college and waited for another chance to be drafted.

So I made the decision to sign. It was a gamble I thought I could win.

The next thing I knew, I was in Kingsport, Tennessee, in the Rookie League. I hoped for the best.

2

Minor and Major

When I was drafted by the Mets, they were a last-place ball club. What pleased me about going to the Mets, however, was that they were a National League team. That gave me the opportunity to play in Los Angeles, and that really excited me.

I had never been to New York. Going there really didn't mean much to me, to be honest about it. I didn't figure that New York would be that different from Los Angeles. I certainly wasn't intimidated by the idea of going to the big city; I had grown up in a big city.

Anyway, I went straight to Kingsport, in Tennessee, to the Mets team in the Rookie

League down there. That was a little strange for me.

I'd never been away from home. I was right out of high school, used to playing ball then going home to be with my mother, my brothers and my sisters. I guess going away from all that for me was sort of like being the little kid who goes off to summer camp for the first time, or a guy who enlists in the army when he's very young and finds himself in basic training, wondering how he got there.

Let me tell you, there's not much to do in Kingsport, Tennessee. When friends from California asked me what I did in Kingsport when I wasn't playing baseball, I said, "nothing." I meant it. I was there to play baseball; I knew that. But I did miss all the things to do that I had in California.

Being away from home, going somewhere to play baseball and not knowing anybody, in a town where you're a stranger, well, that's a test. When you walk down the street, you're not exactly invisible. At least, I wasn't. Everybody knew what I was there to do, but I didn't know anybody I saw on the street. You have to get accustomed to that kind of life style. And that's difficult. You don't know where to go, what to do, who to talk to.

The people who lived in Kingsport were friendly; they knew that we were ball players. I lived in a hotel, a small hotel naturally, with some of the other players. That was wild.

I met other players, of course, guys from other towns, other places in the country, and that was part of my education. I met a pitcher from New York, Al Faust. We'd sit around and talk a lot, and he'd tell me the wild things that happened in New York. Most of the guys on the team were just starting in professional ball. Being away from home was new to most of them, too.

I did have one piece of good luck. I met a guy named Starvin' Marvin. He just came along and introduced himself to me. He knew that I was in a small town, away from home, and that I might be lonely. I was black and he was white. He helped me out, showed me around the town. He wasn't a player, just a friend.

He came to the park one day, said hello, told me he worked at the post office but loved baseball, spent time watching the Kingsport team. He was a friendly guy. We started doing things together. We were a funny look-ing pair; he was short and I was tall. I was young, just out of school; he was about 30. I was black and he was white. But we were a team.

We'd go out and play basketball, catch a

movie, have dinner after the ball games. He helped me adjust. Of course, he couldn't do it all by himself. I had to conquer most of my troubles on my own. (By the way, I still see him; he still lives in Kingsport, but he comes to Atlanta when we're in town.)

Thinking about that time in Kingsport, I guess I was lonely, despite Marvin's best effort to cheer me up. It affected the way I played for Kingsport, too. No question about that.

I never saw the movie *Bull Durham*, but my friends tell me that in those small towns like Kingsport there are those chicks who hang out, who change players every year as the guys move through on their way up. Well, I was there and I don't remember meeting any chicks like that. Not in Kingsport, anyway.

In those days, I spent most of my time playing ball or thinking about playing ball. Chuck Hiller managed the Kingsport team then, and he's a a super guy. When I got there, there was a press conference. Chuck told me he'd never seen that happen before in the Rookie League. I guess it had a lot to do with me playing for New York, where the press does more than just pay attention to you.

Chuck didn't push me. He treated me like

a gentleman. I was calling home almost every day to talk to my mother and my brothers and sisters, and Chuck must have known that I was lonely. I used to hang out outside his door, before games and after games, ready to talk about almost anything he wanted to talk about. I needed his company and he was there for me.

Chuck was a very outgoing person, full of happiness all the time. He wanted to keep his young players happy. He understood what a young player goes through in a situation like that, with so much pressure to make a career in one spectacular season.

He wasn't going to let that happen to me, wasn't going to let anyone destroy me. He was a motivator. He always found time to sit down and talk to me. He'd tell me that there was nothing for me to worry about, that I was going to be a great player. He'd say it was just a matter of hard work and determination. Once you do that, he'd say, you're going to achieve a lot of things.

The press was hanging around, but Chuck kept them off of me. He wanted me to play ball, not sit down for interviews. So Chuck would hold the interviews himself, without me, and answer questions as if he were me.

I learned from Chuck. Sure, I felt lonely and strange. But he never stopped motivating me, trying to give me that little extra drive, to make me play as well as I could.

He promised me that the more I worked, the harder I worked, the better my performance would get. I've confirmed that many times since I played for Chuck. If you have good work habits to begin with, then you'll always achieve what you believe you can achieve.

The next season, 1981, I went up to Lynchburg, Virginia, another small town, not too different from Kingsport. I hadn't done badly at Kingsport. For the season, I batted .268, hit 5 home runs and batted in 20 runs. But that wasn't as good as I could do, I knew. So I was happy to be at Lynchburg.

I guess I hadn't been able to get rid of those demons in my head that made me feel lonely. Early in the season, I still wasn't playing up to my potential. My manager at Lynchburg was Gene Dusan, and he could see that I wasn't doing my best. I guess I was confused. The pressure was on me, and I wasn't yet ready to handle it.

I roomed with Lloyd McClendon, who's now with the Cubs. We had met in the instructional league in Florida, and he had come up to Lynchburg with me. We were in A ball together.

Lloyd told sportswriter William Nack that

I went into a shell and tried to deal with my problems on my own. "He was troubled," Lloyd said. "There were times when he talked about going home. I told him, 'Hang in there. Keep your head on right.' He was young; he didn't have good work habits. In this game, it's easy to stay in bed all day, especially on the road. What Darryl didn't understand is that you have to get your body regulated. You've got to get up early, walk around and do things—go to the mall, take in a movie. It's very easy to lie around and grab a bite and go play. But you're not getting yourself ready either physically or mentally to play the game."

Lloyd was right. I didn't know if I wanted to keep on listening to the press ask if I was ever going to pan out as a great ball player. When I was supposed to be concentrating on playing, I was paying attention to the press. They never really got off my back.

I started thinking I could just get out of there, go to college and play some basketball.

I came real close to doing that. One day in Lynchburg, I got so frustrated that I just didn't show up for the game. I stayed home and said forget it.

The next day there was a story in the paper that I had left Lynchburg, gone back home and didn't want to play baseball anymore.

I had actually just stayed right in Lynchburg. They didn't know if I had really left town or if I was around. The phone kept ringing, but I didn't answer it.

But Gene Dusan was there, and he was a very special guy. Lloyd was my friend; Gene was more like a father. He would bring his sons with the team on the road games, and they would stay in our room. Cutest little kids. We had a great time with them. We used to go out and have dinner with the kids and Gene and his wife. It was wonderful.

He was a considerate and a compassionate man.

But he knew what he had to do. Most of the guys who have helped me during my career had one thing in common—they stayed on my butt, made sure I was really giving all I had.

I've always played the game in a kind of laid-back way. That doesn't mean that I'm not ready to play or that I'm not trying—I am. But the press and others watch me and say, "Wow, he's got so much talent and natural ability, and he's not giving it all."

But that's just the way I've always been. And how can a kid who's 18 or 19 know how good he's going to be? I didn't know.

The only thing you can do is continue to make progress. And when you've got all those people pushing you, like Gene, you drive for it even more.

I listened to Gene. Some people, some players, don't listen. They just sit there and don't think about what's being said. The managers and coaches that you meet when you're young, they want to see you make it big. So I took Gene's words seriously. I felt the things that he said to me.

Gene would tell me to play hard, to be aggressive, never to take anything for granted. I knew what he meant. Sometimes you can't do exactly what's expected of you, but he made me try. That's what counts.

Lloyd taught me, too. He was older than I was, had more baseball experience. Before every game, we'd sit together and talk about the game. We would motivate each other. We'd bet on who'd come out with the most hits.

We'd talk about getting up to the majors, to show time. That's what they call it. Nothing like going to the show, we'd say. Once you've been in the minors and traveled the way we had, when you finally get the call, well, it is show time.

But I knew that I hadn't finished paying my dues.

I hit .255 at Lynchburg, with 13 home runs.

Still not good enough, I thought, but I was ready to move up.

So was Gene Dusan. We were both promoted to the Jackson, Mississippi, team in the Texas League.

I think that the Mets wanted someone who knew me to manage the Jackson team. And Gene knew me so well, the troubles that had surrounded me, the way I was really trying to move on with my life and achieve what I was capable of doing. So Gene came to Jackson, too.

I didn't have any problems in Jackson. It's a university town. I liked that. There were a lot of young people around. There was plenty to do, places to go, good food and more. I had a friend from California who was going to Jackson State, and he took me around. It was a comfortable place, and I felt better there than I had at either Kingsport or Lynchburg.

I was feeling real good about playing professional ball. I came to spring training that year knowing that I was going to double-A ball and knowing that I was going to have a big season. 1982 was going to be a super year for me.

I remember that it was mentioned that I might be brought up by the Mets that year, skipping triple-A. But the Mets executives said no, that I would be destroyed if I was brought up too early. If I had a good year at Jackson, they said, I'd be at Tidewater, triple-A, before the end of the season.

I had a great season at Jackson. I hit 34 home runs, batted in 97 runs and was the league's Most Valuable Player. As Gene said to a reporter, "In Jackson, he just put it all together."

I went to Tidewater for the playoffs in the International League. I was in triple-A and that felt good. Tidewater won the playoffs.

One of my coaches at Jackson, however, was Bobby Valentine, and he remembered something I did during my days at Jackson. Bobby told a magazine writer that in Shreveport that season I dropped a fly ball that cost a run, then came to the plate with two men on.

The crowd was booing me for the error.

"With one swing of the bat, he silenced a crowd like I'd never heard a crowd silenced in my life," Bobby said. "The ball went so high and so far, I was in awe."

Bobby was a very helpful coach. He was one of several guys who worked with me in the minors, who got me to Tidewater on schedule and who helped me make it all the way to Shea Stadium.

He's a very helpful coach, without a lot of motions or noise, the kind who likes you to just go out there and play hard. He lets you go as long as he feels you're doing that.

Bobby doesn't tell you too much. He lets you work on your own when you're on the bases, so you can make things happen. I've been blessed with a lot of good coaches—John Moseley, Brooks Hurst, Chuck Hiller, Gene Dusan, Bobby and others.

In 1983, I went back to Tidewater. I had a great spring in Florida, for the Mets. But they still didn't want to rush me up. I was only 21. So I started out at Tidewater and got off to a hot start. The Mets got off to a terrible start and a month later they called me up.

One thing that may have speeded up the process was the fact that I played winter ball in South America in 1982, after the playoffs at Tidewater. I played in Caracas, Venezuela. It was a tough atmosphere. I didn't speak Spanish, and that was a real problem. I had to learn some of the language and adjust to being in a place like that. I was young, making my way to the majors, and I didn't know what could happen to me down there. I didn't know what it was like to be anywhere but in the United States.

Nothing seriously weird ever happened to me down there; but that doesn't mean that it was an easy experience. One day I hit a home run on the road, and I went back to the outfield at the end of the inning, and the fans started throwing things at me. Bricks, stones. One of our guys came running out to give me a batting helmet. I didn't want it. In fact, I didn't want to go back to the outfield at all. They can get nasty down there.

It was a new experience for me, to be out of the country, and it was the only time I ever did it, but I survived. I hit with power and I played well.

By the way, Davey Johnson was the manager at Tidewater, so I knew him before we were together on the Mets. I got along with him at Tidewater. It was super playing for Davey. In fact, I always got along with Davey, no matter what the press wrote. He's a fun guy. He had certain ways he liked to manage, naturally, and sometimes I didn't approve of the decisions he made, but he was the manager. I never forgot that.

That doesn't mean I didn't get pissed at him. At times, he used the press to complain about me instead of coming to me and telling me what was going on in his head. So we had some shouting matches in the papers.

He got angry with me and I got angry with him. Once I came late to batting practice. I had overslept, in Chicago. And Davey looked at me and told me I wouldn't play that day.

I said, well, if that's how you feel, why don't you just sit me down for a week? And Davey didn't play me for a week.

Eventually, we ended up talking because it was no good for us not to speak to each other. I wasn't saying anything; I wasn't playing. I was just coming to the park. I didn't take batting practice. I was pissed off. Bill Robinson, the Mets coach, would talk to me and tell me to get myself together. You can't be doing this, he'd say to me; the team needs you.

And then I started to think that I was being childish. I told myself to get it together.

I went to Davey and I apologized. And he said, "I can understand what goes through a player's mind. I know that you have problems, a lot of things that you have to deal with. Sometimes you react with all that in your head, and that's what happened to us."

He was right, of course.

But getting back to coming up to the Mets in '83. Some people thought I must have been scared to come up. Not true.

I was a little bit nervous, knowing that it was time to perform at the major league level. I was very pleased to have the chance but a little shocked at the same time. I had spent such a short time at Tidewater, just 16 games, and there I was in the majors. I had the right frame of mind, though, I was with the Mets to do a job.

I had never played a game at Shea Stadium, and the first day I went out to play, I was a starter. I flew into New York that day and played that night. Mario Soto was pitching for the Reds. Soto at that time was one of the top pitchers in the league. He dominated me. I struck out three straight times, then popped up. I remember thinking that I'd never seen pitching like that in the minors.

But I put that in the back of my mind. I would get even, I knew, down the line. It wasn't a personal thing, about me and Soto, at all. I knew he had an advantage, all that major league experience. I gave him credit for having the upper hand, but that would change.

The next year, on opening day in Cincinnati, I hit one off Soto that wound up in the second deck in right field. I did get even.

On that day at Shea in '83, when I first came out on that field to play, there was a lot of excitement inside of me. It had nothing to do with Soto; it had everything to do with being in the major leagues. Here it is, I thought; I'm running onto a major league ball field.

There weren't many people in the stands then, we were a losing ball club. But you still look around and say to yourself, this is it.

The fans really cheered. They were happy to see me up with the Mets. All that cheering couldn't do the job, though. The Mets in '83 were a terrible team.

George Bamberger was the manager when I came up. He was a very quiet man. He'd just fill out the lineup card and tell you to go out there and play, utilize what we had.

Which wasn't much in those days.

George never did say a lot about improving your play. His point was, you're in the majors, just go out there and play. Do your best and everything else will take care of itself.

Well, things didn't take care of themselves, and George resigned. I think he was just tired of it all, the traveling, the headaches of being a manager. He'd had enough.

George had had a heart attack before he became Mets' manager, and I guess he didn't want to have another one. He had a lot to worry about as Mets' manager. Worrying about his heart was enough for one man. Worrying about 24 guys on the ball club and dealing with the press wasn't for him.

Frank Howard, who had been one of the coaches, took over as manager when George left. Frank had a lot of energy. He liked to see you go up there and swing the bat. He was one of those big hitters in his day, so that made sense.

It's hard to define Frank's personality, but I can say that he was the type of gentleman you wanted to stay away from. Frank is a big man, huge. You didn't really want to get too close to him. You stayed away from Frank, just let him do what he felt was right for the ball club. When Frank made a move, you never questioned him about it, not if you were a player.

He was never a critic, though. He was there to help players develop, to help them in any way he could.

Jim Frey was the hitting coach then, and he was very helpful to me. But first I had to need his help.

As things went that year, I needed his help.

After Soto fanned me three times, things didn't get much better. I guess the size of it all got to me: in the majors, all those fans in all those cities, those big parks, your name announced on the loudspeakers. I wanted to do well more than I had ever wanted to do well. I pushed myself. I wanted to hit home runs, to make a good impression on the fans. I didn't stay within myself. I was being fooled by pitchers. I was overswinging, trying to pop the ball out of the park. I thought that I was supposed to be the savior of the team. But I wasn't doing well at that role.

In the middle of June, Frank Howard and Jim Frey decided to bench me. Afterward, remembering that time, I told a sportswriter, "They felt I wasn't putting out enough and they were right. But I didn't know it. I wasn't aware of it. It wasn't attitude. I was struggling, confused. I was thinking of so many things: girlfriend, family, being in the big leagues, going from city to city, new pitchers. I was suddenly in the majors with all these guys I'd been watching for years. Wow! I didn't know where I fit in. It hit me all at one time.

"I didn't know which way to turn, who to turn to, and Frey steps in like a father and says, 'I'm going to help you, but you got to help yourself, too.' I was really green. Frey's a great guy and he really helped me."

Jim was the hitting instructor, and he was the kind of person who was determined to make young players realize that they were capable of playing at the major league level. He motivated me by persuading me not to allow myself to be destroyed by the pressure of being in the majors. He'd tell me that I was there for a reason, that I deserved to be there. That I'd develop my skills even more

50

if I had confidence and believed I could play at the major league level.

I realized, too, that I wasn't relaxing and letting my natural ability take over. I was so upbeat about being in the major leagues that I was trying too hard.

I needed Jim's help. We just used to talk about all sorts of things. He'd say that every time you cross the white line and go out on the field, you have to believe that you're the best player on that field. It doesn't matter who's out there with you, on your team or the opposing team; you have to be sure that you're the best player every time you walk out there.

I started believing what he was telling me, and as I did that, I saw the results. I had more confidence.

As the season went on, I got better and better. I heard Frey's voice: "A lot of good things are going to happen over the next 15 years if you put in the work . . . Study pitchers and get a feel for what each one is trying to do. Baseball can be so much fun if you think of playing in the majors as a gift. Fans and writers are dying to appreciate you and respect you if you just give them a chance . . . Work on your defense . . . A big salary is a player's reward for what he has already done. Most of the players you hold in awe aren't the players they once were . . . Think, 'I'm the best player on the field tonight,' and you will be. Lock that in your head and nobody can take it away."

For weeks during that season, we talked and walked and talked some more. On bus rides, we talked about the game and how important it is to have a mental approach toward the game. Jim's mind is very clear. He communicates what he thinks is important and that means having a winning attitude.

It pleases me that Jim went over to the Cubs and they won the division in '84. We still talk today. He has let me know that he's proud of me, of how I overcame everything. He told me not so long ago that he always believed that I would become the player I am.

The truth is that I got it together in '83. I wound up the season, after that slump, hitting .257, with 26 homers and 74 RBIs.

It was a time of adjustment for me, and it paid off. Fortunately, I didn't have to change my personality along the way.

I've always been the same person, then and now. I've been the kind of person who's very outspoken. I believe in saying nothing but the truth. One of the things I realized after I came up to the majors was that I had to back away from a lot of the media hype. In dealing with the press, I would say things and they would blow them up all out of proportion. I would tell the truth and it would be used against me. The writers knew it was the truth, but other players would be offended.

On the field, I'm less of a pushover now. I don't take anything for granted. I'm more hard-nosed. When I was younger, and a pitcher would hit me intentionally, I would just walk to first base. Well, I got mean about that.

I know that hitting batters will happen. Pitchers don't want you to hit the home run. They get upset. So they brush you off the plate. I can tell the difference now between a guy who wants to hit me and a guy who makes a mistake. When a ball slips out of a guy's hand, you know. When a guy hits you with a straight fast ball, you know that, too.

When you play day in and day out, you learn from experience. Nobody can teach you how to go up there and hit a pitcher who's got certain pitches, for example. Those "schools" develop as you participate. Every time you go out there to play, you see the pitchers, and eventually you know one from another. You start feeling that you can hit some pitchers. You remember that, keep it filed in your mind.

Of course, you can be facing Mike Scott,

and he'll throw that split-finger pitch. Very difficult to hit. It confuses you. You think of so many different things—you face a guy who hadn't had much success in the past, and all of a sudden he comes out and has great success. You wonder where he developed a pitch like that, if he's cheating. Well, if he is cheating, he's doing a good job of it.

You've still got to go out there and face him, so you have to make him the best of it. I've learned not to think about whether or not a guy is cheating. I just worry about going out there and trying to achieve something against him. If you think that a guy is cheating on the mound, you're not going to be successful; he's beaten you before you even step into the box. You might as well give him four at bats and say "you win."

Even the best pitchers, cheating or not, make mistakes. You've got to be ready to capitalize on those mistakes. If the ball doesn't move the way a pitcher wants it to, if you see the ball and you're right on it, you can make something happen.

During that '83 season, at about the All-Star break, I got smart. I had been in the slump, then all of a sudden everything clicked. My approach was to go out and play up to my potential, taking Jim Frey's advice. But Jim couldn't hit for me. I had to do it myself. I put my mind to it and said I was going to come out in the second half of the season and really play. I was going to put all the pieces together.

If you have the tools, attitude makes the difference.

Maybe it just takes time.

It takes time to read a pitcher and get the feel of how he pitches to you. There are times when a guy will pitch to you in a way that's totally different from the last time he pitched against you. You have to be aware of what pitch you're likely to get in a certain situation.

The good pitchers change around. They don't pitch to you the same way at each at bat.

Good pitchers are the ones who try to mix their pitches really well, keep you off balance. When you're young, as I was coming up in '83, it's hard to be a patient hitter. Young hitters get anxious. They want to swing at everything. But once you develop patience, you can look for your pitches to hit. You let the others just go by, and you look for the ones that you think you're capable of doing something with.

So I wound up having a good year in '83. And I'm careful not to feel sorry for that team the Mets fielded that season. I wasn't the only player trying to do his best.

George Foster, for example, went out there every day and tried hard. He was a very religious person, a quiet guy. He'd just go about his business and try to perform at his best. He had a good year in '83, in fact. He hit 28 home runs and batted in 90 runs that season even though we finished last. He had signed a big package deal with the Mets, after all of his fine years at Cincinnati, and the pressure was on him. Millions of dollars. He was being paid to deliver, and he did.

George got along with everybody, but there was some jealousy among some of the other players about the kind of money he was making. Sour jokes. No insults to George's face, just a few bitter jokes.

George was a loner, anyway. He spent his free time with his family. A lot like me in that sense. And I got along with him.

We had others who weren't as retiring.

Dave Kingman, now he was a strange character. He didn't talk much either. He had his own style. Nobody wanted to say too much to Kingman because with that name, he reminded us of King Kong. Big as he was, he could destroy you at any time. He was bigger than I was. Dave Kingman was huge. And a lot of guys on the team told me that Dave did some strange things, such as the day a lady reporter came into the locker room and Dave had a box with a dead rat in it and he gave it to her. He told her he had something he really wanted her to have. She opened it up, and there was the dead rat. She won't ever forget that.

Rusty Staub was on that team, too. We had two managers that season, Bamberger and Howard, but Rusty was sort of a manager as well. He would be very helpful to the young players. He knows hitting, did then and probably still does. So he filled us in with a lot of good points.

Rusty was a left-handed hitter, and so am I. He would tell me how to pick up a curve ball from a pitcher he'd faced often, which part of the zone to look in, how to know when the pitcher makes a mistake, so you can get the bat head on it and hit it a long way.

Most important to me and those of us who wanted the Mets to improve, Keith Hernandez arrived in '83. Keith has his own ways, his own personality, his own style. When he arrived, the press named him as the main guy on the team, and he liked that. He played the press extremely well. There were times when he would use his advantage with the press against his teammates.

He'd tell the press, "I don't think this guy's

doing well enough," and that would appear in the paper.

The press wants stories, conflicts. They don't care about team solidarity. It gets them off to write negative things. When there's a problem on a team, the players ought to talk about it, among themselves, not to the press. That's why there's a team captain, to call a meeting if there's a need for one.

Of course, in reality there aren't many meetings like that. Most guys just go about their business.

The next season, 1984, marked a turn for the better for the Mets, and for me.

The previous October, after the '83 season, Davey Johnson became manager. And we got a new young pitcher, Dwight Gooden.

I became Doc's friend right away. I didn't know him in the minors, but I'd heard a lot of good things about him. He'd gone to spring training and he just dominated. Davey decided to keep him on the team for the regular season. He was just 19, and some of the team executives wanted to send him down to triple-A, but Davey insisted on keeping him.

Doc thinks when he pitches; he doesn't just throw. He's a very smart pitcher. He thinks about where he wants to put the ball. He's very disciplined on the mound. It's hard for any pitcher who comes up that young, but Doc had poise and confidence then as he has now; he knows what he's capable of doing.

I was encouraged when he came up. The team was bound to improve. We had Ron Darling, too, another outstanding pitcher. I could see a turnaround for the club that season.

Mookie Wilson also played an important role in '84. He's a low-key kind of guy, just goes out there to have fun. He plays hard, does his job without a lot of complaining. He hit .276 in '84, with 10 home runs and 46 stolen bases. Not shabby.

It was a year of improvement for us. We finished second to the Cubs in our division, going 90–72. It was the second-best record in Met history. Doc won the Rookie of the Year award. He went 17–9, with 276 strikeouts, a rookie record. He averaged more than 11 strikeouts per nine innings.

Hernandez, whatever our differences may have been, knows how to play the game. He hit .311 in '84, drove in 94 runs and won another golden glove, his seventh straight. He knows all the aspects of the game. When you play with him, you have to respect his skills.

I led the club in home runs, with 26, and RBIs, with 97.

Rusty was still with us, and he led the

league in pinch hits (18) and pinch RBIs (18). Jesse Orosco had 31 saves.

Four guys—Hernandez, Gooden, Orosco and me—were named to the league's All-Star team. It was an honor that was to happen to me again after that, but I'll never forget the first time.

It was a good year. Better ones were ahead of us. We were learning how to win and how to have fun doing it.

Jesse Orosco was a good teacher. He was a very funny guy, loose, a super guy. He was one of the guys in a group we called the scum bunch. We'd all sit in the back of the plane, with our music blasting loud, drinking beer, just having a ball. We had food fights, too, you name it.

In '84, we had Walt Terrell on the team; he got traded to Detroit after that season. He was a wild guy. He'd get on the loudspeaker on the plane and make some weird and funny announcements, about the manager and the front-office people.

In '85, our team continued to improve. We finished second again, but our record was better, 98–64. Doc won the Cy Young award; he went 24–4, the youngest 20-game winner in modern history.

Gary Carter came from Montreal and led the club with 32 homers and 100 RBIs. It was a pleasure to play with Gary. There was excitement about his arrival. Here was another guy coming over who was well established. The team was starting to blend into an outstanding club.

Gary has been blessed by the Lord in so many ways. He's very dedicated to his work on the field, and he's just as dedicated to his work off the field. I think that something really touched his heart when his mother died of leukemia. He became a spokesman for those who are doing research in that disease, and he's raised a lot of money to fight it.

Gary's very involved, on and off the field. He shows you what a real professional is. He's very helpful to everybody, doesn't criticize anyone. He stands for a long time signing autographs. That's not a bother for him; it's a pleasure.

In '85, Hernandez hit over .300, won another gold glove and had 24 game-winning RBIs.

I missed seven weeks with a thumb injury, but still hit 29 homers.

Ron Darling went 16–6 and Sid Fernandez went 9–9, but had a 2.80 ERA. Orosco and Roger McDowell were responsible for 34 saves, 17 each.

Four of us—Carter, Gooden, Darling and me—made the All-Star team.

We fought the battle in '85 down to the last day of the season, when St. Louis won it.

And in '85, we had a home attendance of 2,751,437. It not only broke the old mark; it was a record for New York City major league baseball.

Roger McDowell kept the flake tradition alive with the Mets. It's no secret that relief pitchers are a different breed. They have a lot of time to think out there and a lot of energy. McDowell had all kinds of gimmicks. He came up in '85, but one of his greatest flake achievements came the next year.

That was the year that he and Howard Johnson came up with the hot foot. They put a cigarette together with gum and matches and lit it. They'd sneak up and stick the hot foot on you. You wouldn't know, of course, and suddenly the thing would go off and you'd jump like mad.

They'd do it during a game, too. They used to get coach Bill Robinson all the time. He'd be in the first base coach's box, and the thing would spark up, and he'd kick his feet and go running.

Roger was just a character. He'd show up with all the costume masks he'd collected, all kinds of ugly animals, and he'd go around in his uniform with a mask on. Once, in Philadelphia, he wore roller skates on the field, during batting practice. In Chicago before a game he'd borrow a hose from the grounds crew and cool off the fans in the bleachers. Fans began by thinking of Roger as a nasty Met. But on those hot summer days in Chicago, they thanked him.

In '86 we won it all, and there's no feeling like that one. Even the statistics for that year still get me excited when I read them. We won our division with a 108–54 record, leading it by 21½ games. The team hit 148 homers; I hit 27 and had 93 RBIs and a slugging average of .507. We were ahead in the east from April 23.

Gary Carter had 105 RBIs. Hernandez won another gold glove and hit .310. Gooden was 17–6; Fernandez was 16–6. Darling's ERA was 2.81. Bob Ojeda, who we got from Boston, was 18–5 with a 2.57 ERA.

Five of us made the All-Star team: Carter, Hernandez, Gooden, Fernandez and me. We won the league title, four games to two over Houston. Then we won the World Series against Boston in seven games, after losing the first two games at home. In game six we were one out away from losing it all but won it 6–5 in ten innings. Then we won it all with a come-from-behind 8–5 win in game seven.

In that famous game six, we were tied in the tenth inning when a ground ball went through Bill Buckner's legs. Maybe I should say that some of us felt sorry for Buckner, letting us find new life at that point in a crucial game. But I can't. We felt happy. It was one of those miracle things that happen in this game.

Think about it. Boston went with a guy who had been there all year. You don't just take him out at that point in the game. The ball could have been hit to the second baseman or the shortstop. Anything could have happened. What did happen was good for us. You won't hear me complaining.

It was a great season. We won those 108 games, and most of the credit should go to the biggest surprise of all, Bobby Ojeda. He was the real dominant force for us in '86. He won the big games that we had to win in the playoffs, against the Astros, and he also won the big games that we had to win in Boston. We went to Boston down 2–0, and he won the third game.

Of course, we all had a good year.

Then, in '87, we had a letdown, a drop-off, from all that excitement. We finished second at 92–70. I had 39 home runs, 104 RBIs, 36 stolen bases, and I hit my best average in the majors, .284. But it wasn't enough to inspire us to repeat what we did in '86.

Hernandez won another gold glove, his tenth in a row. But our pitchers suffered; they spent a total of 457 days on the disabled list.

But no season is a total loss. Lenny Dykstra was hustling all season. Kevin McReynolds joined the team. Tim Teufel hit .308. Howard Johnson was there.

Hojo likes to have a lot of fun. So does Dykstra. Dykstra's gone now, over to Philadelphia, but when he was with us a lot of people thought he was cocky. Well, look at him. Look at his size. The man has to believe in himself if he's going to play up here and play the way he can. He has to be a hard-nosed player. And that's what he is. His style is like what Pete Rose's must have been when he came up. Rolling hard, diving for balls.

McReynolds is a little like George Foster. Quiet. Laid-back. He doesn't say much; he collects his pay and does his job. He's from Arkansas, and he likes to hunt in the off-season, shoot deer.

Teufel got busted in Houston in '87. A bar fight. He was out with the boys that night. We were all out. I left early, because I had to play the next day and I thought those guys were getting a little bit out of hand. The next thing I heard about it was when somebody called me at five o'clock in the morning and said the guys had been arrested and were going to jail unless someone bailed them out.

Teufel, Darling, Ojeda, Aguilera—they were involved. When something like that happens and you're with your teammates, you defend each other. You jump in.

I heard that Tim had had a little bit too much to drink. The place was closing up, and he told the guy to play more music or something like that and that he had some beer left to drink. The guy told him it was time to go.

Okay, you know you're in Houston, right? And it's time to go and they tell you to go. So you leave your beer there and you go on about your business. But Tim tried to walk out with the beer, and the guy told him he couldn't do that. They got into a shoving match, and before anybody knew it, guys were on Tim and our guys joined in to help him.

But that's the kind of season '87 was. Things didn't go the way we wanted them to go. Jesse Orosco asked to be traded. I had some exchanges with other players. The fans booed Gary Carter. Mookie Wilson asked to be traded. Wally Backman and I almost got into the ring before we realized that boxing wasn't our sport.

Worst of all: St. Louis played better than we did and won it.

We improved in '88. Much of the mean stuff vanished. We got down to business. Everybody thought we'd win our division, and we did. Everybody said we'd win the National League title, and we thought we would. But we didn't.

We went 100–60 and finished first by 15 games. I hit 39 homers to lead the league. I had 101 RBIs, too. Our pitchers led the league. David Cone was 20–3, with an ERA of 2.22 and 213 strikeouts. Doc won 18 and Ron Darling won 17. The bull pen had 46 saves, thanks to Randy Myers and Roger McDowell. We led the league in homers, runs scored and on-base percentage.

And we lost to the Dodgers four games to three in the National League Championship Series.

Hershiser won the seventh game in L.A. with a 6–0 five-hitter. And that was it.

Many people have said to me that we were the better team on paper, if not on the field. Sure. It didn't do us much good, because the game is played on the field. We may have been the better team, but we didn't win and the Dodgers did. Maybe it was the desire that they showed in every game. Maybe we took too much of it for granted. It's hard to know. What mattered was that we lost.

When that happens, you lick your wounds and try to get ready for next season.

That's what I did.

3

Friends,
Foes and Heroes

You start out in spring training and you go through the regular season and past it to the playoffs and the World Series. That's most of the year. You can't get through it without getting to know the guys on your team. At least you get to know those who want you to know them. There are some guys who are private, who go about their business and don't say much. They do what they're paid to do. Or they don't and then they disappear—to the minors, to other teams, into retirement.

Whether you win it all in any given year, or lose, may depend on how the guys get along. When there's unity, there's strength.

In recent years, I've gotten to know the guys on the Mets. I can't say that there's one I don't like, whatever the press has reported.

Let me run down a few here.

Rick Aguilera is a very quiet guy from California. He was born there and still lives there. He's had his troubles. In 1988 he had surgery on his right elbow; before that, he'd been in pain. But he came back, in his determined way. He pitched well in the league championship series against the Dodgers. His ERA was 1.29. He does his job and cares about it, but it's hard to know what Rick is thinking. He keeps things to himself. Now he's with Minnesota.

David Cone's the opposite. He's a very funny, open person. He came over to the Mets from Kansas City in 1987, and even though he was born in Kansas City and lived there when he was traded, he responded well to the guys on the Mets. He thinks we're all buddies, a great group. And he's part of that. When a guy does that, comes over from the other league, and does it as well as David has, the guys on the team are glad for him and glad for the team. We pull for each other. The pitching staff has solidarity. They never push each other to the side.

What some people don't remember about David is that he broke the little finger of his right hand, his pitching hand, in '87. He overcame that and became a 20–3 pitcher for us in '88.

Terry Leach, who got traded in mid–1989, was one of the older guys on the team, one of the veterans, at 35. He was into his own thing. He spent a lot of years in the minors, and he survived and went on to do well with us. All the guys on the club liked him and respected him. He wasn't loud, with a lot to say, he didn't brag about anything. He was just a real professional. A lot of guys wouldn't have made it through what Terry went through. In the minors, he played for Baton Rouge, Greenwood, Savannah, Kingston, Richmond, Jackson and Tidewater—some of them more than once—and he spent parts or all of six seasons with the Mets. He paid his dues, and the guys who played with him appreciated that.

Randy Myers, traded in '89, was the real psycho of the club. He was one of those guys who think they've been on duty in Vietnam. He was born in 1962, so he'd have to have been the youngest guy ever to go into combat. He wore those Vietnam shirts and acted like an infantry grunt. His locker was next to mine, and I talked to him all the time, but from where I stood, he was crazy. He thought he was in combat when he played baseball.

Here's a guy who went out to the mound with a knife in his pocket.

You'd ask him, "Well, Randy, what's the knife for?"

He'd go, "See, you never know what might happen. If a guy charges me, I'll slice his throat."

You wonder about a guy like that.

On the other hand, he did save games for us. In '88, he converted 26 of 29 save opportunities. He knew what he was doing on the mound. He could get guys out without the knife.

On the subject of pitchers, Bobby Ojeda is one of my favorite guys on the team. He's funny and he's smart, a good combination of ingredients. He's one of the original scum bunch. And talk about tough. He almost lost the upper portion of his left middle finger in an accident with a hedge clipper in the fall of '88. Surgery was done by the Mets' doctors, Dr. Richard Eaton and Dr. James Parkes. They put the finger together again, but it was on his pitching hand. No one knew for sure if Bobby would be able to pitch again, or how well he would pitch. Well, Bobby knew. He worked at it and came back all the way. It was almost a miracle, a miracle helped along by the guy's toughness, his desire to achieve.

That's an example he set for every player who's ever been hurt.

Our pitcher from Hawaii, Sid Fernandez, has had his struggles, but he always works hard. It seems that we can't come up with the big runs for him. He doesn't give up many hits or many runs. But he'll get himself in a situation where he'll walk one or two and then he'll give up the big home run. He'll wind up losing the game 3–2 or something like that because we didn't give him enough support.

When you give up a home run after you walk a guy or two, I think it's more of a mental problem. Sid isn't yet at the stage that Doc Gooden is. If Doc walks one or two guys, the next guy is going to eat dust. He'll go right at him. Maybe Sid isn't angry enough, doesn't have that fire in him that would get him pissed enough to say, the next guy I'm going to eat alive.

But people are from different breeds. His style is a laid-back old-fashioned one, not the aggressive approach you sometimes need. Some have that extra drive, like the challenge. I like to be in that pressure situation, as a matter of fact. If you feel you're the best, you have to feel you're the best at a specific time.

There are guys on the team, younger guys,

who don't have the confidence yet to believe that they are good enough that they can do this, do that. Doc could teach them all about that. He is a Hall of Fame pitcher.

Doc and I are good friends. But even a good friend doesn't always know what's going on in a guy's head. When Doc had his drug problem, I couldn't really tell that he had one. Thinking back on it, maybe some of us should have guessed. There were signs. Maybe after a game on the road, we'd ask Doc if he wanted to go out to dinner, and he'd ask us where we were going to be and say he'd be there or he'd call our rooms. We'd wait and wait and we'd check with him and he'd say, "I'll meet you there," but he'd never show up.

It made me think, finally, that he was in trouble.

What makes all of his teammates and fans and his family very happy is that he defeated that habit the way he wins games—by his concentration, his determination, his mental toughness. And, of course, his talent ought to take him wherever he wants to go. Some people say that Doc is too quiet, but he's not that quiet with his friends. And I'm happy to be one of his friends.

That confidence, that's what young players need to have. It takes some guys a little longer to get it. In baseball, as in all things, you have to realize how good you really are and what you're capable of doing before you can succeed.

Whatever problems Gregg Jefferies has had, especially in early '89 after he had that great time at the end of '88, he's no fluke. He's in the situation that I was in. I can understand what he went through. A lot was expected of him. That creates pressure, and too much pressure early on is bad for your nerves.

He played in spring training with us in '88, and he had been sent down to triple-A. He got off to a real tough start down there. He had all that media coverage because he'd been one of the top players in the minor leagues for two or three years. They were writing about how great he was going to be and finally it hit him. He pressed and tried too hard.

At one point during the season, we went down to Tidewater to play their team, and I got together with Gregg. I told him that there was no reason for him to worry about the pressure. I told him to play the way he was capable of playing, because eventually he'd come up to the Mets and find a slot with us. It was just a matter of time. Once he did come up, toward the end of '88, he wound up in the lineup as I knew he would.

Gregg made the best out of the opportunity. He did a super job for us, and he never had a big head about it. There's no reason to be arrogant when you feel you can play well.

The truth is that when you get up to the majors, it's a lot easier to play. The competition is great and that brings out the best in you. That's when you start believing in yourself, even if you hadn't done it before. That's what happened to Gregg. He got here and he performed at the level he always wanted to perform at.

I have no doubts that he'll make it up here.

Dave Magadan has a lot of talent, too. He's not one of the lively guys, however. He's another of the quiet, low-key kind, like McReynolds and Aguilera. They don't have much to say. They're not really a part of the social system on the team.

Keith Miller, on the other hand, is relatively new to the club, but he's an exciting young kid. Fun to be with. He plays hard and he's determined to do well. He's not a flake, either. Keith is young, just 25, and he's on a team that has its share of experienced guys. At 27, just two years older than Keith, I feel like I'm one of the veterans.

Of course, there's a time when you know it's going to be over soon. That can be painful, especially if you're not ready to leave, if you think there's more for you to achieve. It's hard to give up on that. But you have to know that there are young players coming up. You have to make room for them.

Mookie Wilson was another veteran, at 33, but it seemed to me that when the Mets traded him, Mookie had a lot left to give the game. He's a true professional. He's never had much to say in public or to the press, but when it's time to play, he goes out there and does the job, without complaining.

When I say these things about the team and the players on it, I know that every guy plays his role. But among the guys who play every day, there have been three of us who've been at the core of what motivated the Mets during the eighties.

I like to think I'm one of the guys who kept the engine running. So was Gary Carter. He's been playing pro ball since 1972. He had all those great years with Montreal, and when he came to the Mets in '84, he brought that inspirational quality with him. I feel that I'm lucky to have been on the team with him. He wants to win and he gives you that message all the time. And it's not just words that he passes out. He plays, too, on a very high level, even when he's hurt.

Keith Hernandez and I had our differences. I guess that's well known by now. But if we disagreed, we made up not long afterward. That ought to be well known, too, but it isn't.

The press tried to picture us as enemies, but that hasn't worked, because it's just not true. Keith is a true leader. He was in St. Louis, he was with the Mets, and I'll bet he will be with Cleveland. He leads on the field, keeps the pitcher's mind on the game, keeps the infield together. He has guys thinking the way they should think. He'll tell guys how to play and he knows what he's talking about. He gives the pitcher that extra motivation, tells the pitcher things like "You can get this guy out. Pitch him this way." That's a big help. You need that extra kick when you're struggling. Keith's a big motivator in the dugout, too. We got some deal when we got him, in 1983, for pitchers Neil Allen and Rick Ownbey.

It's not too tough to go out on the field with guys like those I've mentioned here. When we're all healthy and all available at the same time, the Mets are tough to beat. Some of the older guys will retire in time and some young ones will come up to take their places, but I won't forget what it was like to play with the Mets in the eighties.

One aspect of the game I'll remember, because I'm best known as a hitter, is the way

I've had to learn to face some of the best pitchers in the game.

I was reading a baseball magazine before the '89 season, and I saw a list of the ten top hitters in baseball. I was on it, but most of the others—except for Tony Gwynn and Andre Dawson—were from the American League. The American League is more of a hitters' league. I haven't been to all the parks in that league, but I understand that they are smaller than the National League parks. In the National League, the pitchers can, and do, dominate.

There are some tough pitchers in our league.

In '88, the toughest was Orel Hershiser. I had to adjust when I faced him. I had to be patient, very selective. I had to look for a pitch in a certain spot. It depended upon the situation, of course, because if there were runners on base, I looked for a pitch I could just drive.

You don't go up to the plate and try to kill the ball in every situation. It depends, as I noted, on several things. How many runs do we have? How many runs do they have? What inning is it? You have to know what to look for in certain situations.

Hershiser pitched to me very carefully. He tried to get me to chase a lot of bad pitches.

That's the good pitchers' rule: If you don't have to throw a hitter a good pitch, don't throw him one. If you make a mistake throwing a good hitter a good pitch, he's going to capitalize on it.

A good hitter must know the strike zone. Once you learn that, you know what you're doing. And the only way to learn it is to discipline yourself, to analyze it. Sometimes you just sit at home at night and think about the strike zone. How big is it? You mark out a plate on the floor and stare at it. That's what makes you a better hitter, when you sit down and teach yourself about the game.

Of course, you still run into the trouble with the umpire's version of the strike zone. You have to make adjustments for that. You have to watch each umpire very carefully, figure the way he's calling the game. You have to start at the very beginning of the game to get a fix on it.

Sometimes you may have to donate a time at bat to find out, but you don't want to do that. Every at-bat is important to me now, and that first time up in a game is very important. It sets up your whole game; you find out if you're on the ball.

It's a mind game to a degree.

Take Danny Jackson. He had a good year with Cincinnati in '88. He was a big surprise to a lot of us, because he hadn't pitched in the National League before. We hadn't seen him, so we didn't know what he threw.

He's one of those pitchers who has a hard cutter, a pitch that runs into right-handers and away from left-handers. Danny's a left-hander who's difficult to hit off of, whether you're right-handed or left-handed. Maybe that's why he had such a good year. Some of us in the National League will figure him out, though, if we have enough time to do it.

I've had good luck against left-handers. It's got a lot to do with my confidence. There was an old theory that left-handed batters didn't hit left-handed pitchers. I said to myself that the only way I was going to hit left-handers was to go up there and believe I could hit them. I got up on the plate and made them throw pitches they thought they could get me out with, and I showed them that they couldn't.

Then there's Mike Scott. His pitches sometimes do strange things. For him, you've got to be prepared. Just to see the ball. And you've got to hope that he makes a mistake. When a pitcher like Scott is having a great year, the only way you're going to beat him is if he makes mistakes. That's the name of the game. If he doesn't make any mistakes, you just tip your cap to him and say he had a wonderful night. That's part of this business. You're not going to be a winner every night.

But you should be ready. What I mean is that if you've seen a guy's best pitch, if you know what it is, and then he comes with that pitch, you can get a hold of it. Maybe you alter your swing a little to get it—a nice, short, quick swing, maybe.

I've batted against Rick Reuschel often. Some fans look at him and think he's pitching from a chair. You look at him and you think he's got nothing going for him. He's overweight and slow, or so you think. That's how he gets you. Because he's smart and he's mastered the way he pitches. He's a thinking man. He knows when a batter can beat him and he's not going to give that guy a pitch that will let him. People wonder how he can go from one team to another—Chicago, Pittsburgh, San Francisco—and still win wherever he is. Fifteen, sixteen games. It's because he uses his head. He's not a seriously gifted pitcher. But when you master something, it's like being the captain of a plane; he knows how to fly. Rick Reuschel has mastered pitching.

Rick Sutcliffe of the Cubs is another pitcher who knows what he's doing. When I faced him, when he first came to Chicago, he impressed me. He has a very smooth delivery, with a graceful style. He makes good pitches and mixes them very well. He knows how to get hitters out.

I believe that I can hit anybody's best fast ball, but some pitchers can still give you trouble, even with the fast ball. You have to be as smart as the pitcher, if you can. You have to know how to hit a breaking ball. You have to be able to hit any pitch that comes up there. I feel I can do that if I'm looking for the ball in a certain zone.

That doesn't mean that I'm getting ready to bat 1.000. As the sportscasters like to say, if you get three hits out of ten official at-bats, you're a star. So the pitcher has the advantage every time you go out on the field. You try to cut that advantage, to do what you want to do some of the time. Just that much will win games, create big innings.

Nolan Ryan has given me trouble; Nolan Ryan has given everybody trouble. He can be overpowering, even after all his years on the mound. I don't feel bad about being another name in his book. I have a lot of company.

There are other pitchers around who can give you trouble, too, of course.

Joe Magrane shows some promise, but he's had his troubles. It's too early to tell. He can be very tough at certain times, but sloppy at others.

Some relief pitchers get my attention. Mark Davis, with San Diego, to name one. He's a left-hander, and he's got a real good breaking ball and a good fast ball. Davis and other relief pitchers have an advantage. You've been facing one guy until late in the game, and then they bring in a new guy, a top reliever out of the bull pen. You may beat the guy, but the majority of the time a stopper stops you. That's what he's there to do. John Franco did a super job at Cincinnati. He's got good pitches and he knows how to mix them up—I'm looking forward to playing with him now that he's a Met.

Jim Gott and Todd Worrell inspire bad dreams, too.

It's important to know that speed is not the only quality that a reliever has to have, especially if you've faced a guy who throws junk for six innings. Then, any reliever seems fast. You have to put up your dial a little bit, to be ready to deal with that.

Some pitchers, starters mostly, are just plain smart. That's their strength. I think of John Tudor in that category. He's a very intelligent pitcher. Finesse. That's what he's got. He tries to make you chase his pitch, and he's very good at that. At times you will. He'll play a little game with you. He'll throw pitches in a certain way, then all of a sudden he'll try to sneak a fast ball in on you. And you know that on the next pitch, he'll throw one of those slow change-ups to make you fish for it outside. He'll get you out that way.

Bob Knepper's a big guy, a sidewinder, with a big, slow curve. He's a little like Tudor. He's a left-hander who doesn't throw hard, not as hard as Tudor can when he wants to, but he'll make you chase bad balls. A veteran pitcher, in other words. That's saying that he's a smart pitcher. Those pitchers won't throw you a strike unless they have to. They figure, well, this guy is up there free-swinging, and there's no need to throw a strike because he's going to be swinging anyway.

If you don't swing, a pitcher like that will fall behind in the count or even walk you before he'll give you a good pitch to hit. A smart pitcher would rather give you the free base than let you destroy one off of him.

As a hitter, I look at other hitters, too. Not to learn from them, really, but to admire the way they hit. I can be on the bench or in right field and still know when a guy's playing the game as well as it can be played. I'm not sure I have heroes, but there are some guys who do inspire me.

One of the players I admire most is Ozzie Smith. He's another true professional who's done a great job in his career. It's easy for me to call him one of the best players in the game. It's exciting, even for me playing against him, to see the kinds of things he does at shortstop.

I happen to know him personally. We talk a lot and he's always open and kind. He's invited me over for dinner when we're in St. Louis; he's a generous guy. He's also the best infielder I've ever seen. I've never seen anyone make the plays he makes.

Among outfielders, Andre Dawson is excellent. He's a terrific outfielder who knows what he's doing. He knows the bases, too, and he's very strong. They call him "The Hawk," and they should. He's tough and strong and fast. And quiet.

Tony Gwynn, he's another fine outfielder. And so is Eric Davis, at Cincinnati. Dale Murphy's another, a pro who's put in all those years with a ball club that's never been at the top, but has given his best all that time. That's hard to do and as a man, he's a clean living sort of person.

Kirk Gibson of the Dodgers is a great guy. A down-to-earth person who's intense on the field and gives you no trouble off the field. He's out to win, and that's what it takes in this business. You want to have fun with what you do, but you want to go out there to win.

Andres Galarraga, at Montreal, is one of the finest young players in the game today. He's a great fielder for his size, and an outstanding hitter. He hits both home runs and for average. He drives in a lot of runs and he gets a lot of extra-base hits.

I played against Andy Van Slyke in the minors, when he was with a Cardinal team in Arkansas. He was a fine player down there and he still is. He never really blossomed into what the Cardinals thought he ought to be, I guess. But at Pittsburgh, he's come into his own. I'm not surprised. Sometimes it takes some players a little longer to develop. Sometimes it takes a change of scene as well.

I admire Vince Coleman, too. He uses his head. That's the key to his game. He's not a super hitter, but he gets on base, and he gets there by utilizing his speed. Many fast guys don't know how to do what he does, and once you master what Vince has mastered, it makes you a very special player. It gets you 20 infield hits a year. He sets the tone of the game, and he can change it, too. He sets it by getting on base, and he changes it by stealing second. He hits a ground ball and he winds up with a double. I like that.

Those are guys who are playing today. I also have a lot of respect for a couple of guys who aren't playing right now, who've retired.

Mike Schmidt has had a big impact on the game: the way he played, the way he carried himself, his entire career. Once, early in my career with the Mets, I was having some trouble and I had several talks with him that cleared my head. He made me feel better about myself, and that helped my game. I won't forget that.

Pete Rose is another one who inspired me. He didn't have one of the best bodies in the game and he wasn't one of the most talented players, but you watch him play and you know all you have to know about desire. He had that desire in his heart, to go out there day after day and play hard. How can you not admire somebody like that? He had a teammate who played that same way, Joe Morgan. A lot of little guys have big hearts. I admire that. Big guys like me, who have talent, raw natural ability, we can get up there and hit the ball out of the park and play well, run well, all of it. Those little guys don't have all that going for them, but the way they play they make it seem like they've got everything you've got.

Ty Cobb must have been like that. Rose broke his record, so he's probably like Cobb was. I mean, if you're going to take out the second baseman, really take him out. Rose ran right over a catcher in an All-Star game. Ran him over. Messed up his career. It was part of the game the way Rose played it—to win.

When Rose was having all of that trouble over his gambling, there really wasn't that much talk about it among the players I know. We understood his situation. The man had his own life to live. Whatever he did outside of baseball, that was his life, his money. If he wanted to bet on horses, okay.

Of course, betting on, or against, your own team is another matter. I'm not one to say he did that. How can you be a manager and bet against your own club? You'd blow the game yourself.

That's serious.

But baseball isn't always serious. There are times when it's relaxed, even times when it's funny.

On TV, you see a guy get to first base and it looks like he's talking to the first baseman. Well, he is doing just that. We talk to most of them.

We don't have heavy conversations or get distracted from the game, but when there's a pause, we talk. Guys will say, "Hey, you're looking great. You must be having a great year." Some first basemen will congratulate you: "Keep up the good work." I'll say the same to them.

Will Clark, at San Francisco, talks too much. He gets on your nerves. Every time I get to first base, he peeks at me and says, "What's up, slugger?" Or he'll say, "I see you're still hitting them out of the park." I say, "Well, I'm trying. I'm trying to be just like you."

Pedro Guerrero is another funny one.

I'll go to first, and I'll say, "Pete, man, you're going to have to play me in next time, because if you play me way back there, I'm going to bunt."

And he says, "Go right ahead, bunt it. Because if the ball comes this way, I'm going to throw it at you. I'm not going to get killed picking up that bunt."

Some catchers talk to you, but most of them keep quiet. They've got to concentrate. Tony Pena, he talks a lot. He uses a Spanish word that means ugly. "You're ugly," he says, in Spanish. He jokes around before you get into the box. He tries to make you laugh. I just drop my head, so he can't see my face.

I speak to the umpires all the time. They're friendly. A number of them have talked to me and have told me they respect the way I play the game. They've told me that they like the way I've handled myself, with all the trials I've had. Some have told me that they want me to keep up my good work, because I will have a super career.

There are a couple of first-class umpires in the National League. That doesn't mean that the rest of them are no good. It just means that several stand out. John McSherry is a good umpire. That means, to me, that he's consistent. If he calls a pitch a strike in the first inning, he'll call that same pitch a strike in the eighth inning. Doug Harvey is a fair umpire. He's got his own style. We call him The Lord. He's the sort of umpire who doesn't argue with you. He feels that everything he says is right. McSherry doesn't argue much, either, but that's because he's low-key. He just does his job and calls the game.

The truth is there's no good reason for a player to get into an argument with an umpire. Once the call is made, he's not going to change it. It's never happened yet and it's not going to happen.

Once in a while, an umpire will blow a call. Say he's missed a ball, called it a strike. The next time I'm up, I might say, "Don't you think that was a little low?"

"It probably was," the ump might say. "I blew that one."

"Don't worry about it" is what I say to that.

They'll make it up to you if you don't show them up.

Eric Gregg, he's a funny umpire. A huge guy, a likeable guy, he does all kinds of funny stuff. When he's behind the plate, he keeps up a string of little orders: "All right. Come on. Let's go. Shake it up." I feel like saying to him, "What's up, you got a date after the game?" The guys in the dugout might shout, "Yes, he's got a date with a steak and potatoes."

Generally, the umpires do try to keep away from the players. They don't have dinner with the players. I wouldn't want to do that even if I could. That'd be crossing the line.

There are other kinds of experiences in this game, as well. I've been in a bunch of All-Star games. That's something you dream about. It's a hard feeling to express, that desire, the achievement itself. Sometimes it's hard to believe that you're at that point in your career where so many people recognize you and select you to the All-Star game. What really makes me feel good is that the media have often tried to write me off, but the people never have. They know what kind of a player I really am.

It's hard to describe the feeling when you show up to play in that game. We play against each other all the time, and there's respect among us, and then there we are, playing on the same team. You don't have to be too serious about it, because everybody on the team knows it's an event that we're all there to enjoy.

You do try to win, of course. But you remember it for the friends you've made, as well, from your own league and from the other one.

That's just one of the wonderful things about baseball: making friends.

4

The Post-Season Season

When the regular season ends, another season begins.

Not immediately, of course. It's tough trying to get from spring training to October without injuries, distractions, whatever. If you do, the first thing that comes to your mind is to sit back and relax, forget about baseball.

It's what I'd call a return to ordinary life. No waking up in the morning to get ready to play; I have the right to sleep in if that's how I feel. That's what I do first of all.

You can get used to that, believe me. I know that once I let myself relax, it takes a lot of self-motivation to get going again. That means getting up knowing you have to work out, start riding your cycle again, just to get the juices flowing.

For a long time now, I've been working with Keith Cedro, who's the Mets strength and conditioning coach. Keith has worked with college athletes, at Seton Hall, and with the New York Giants football team. He designs workouts for us. His workouts are aimed at improving flexibility. He has us doing moderate weight-lifting and aerobics programs.

I've got a bunch of equipment in my basement at home in New York, and I work on it after the season. Sometimes, Keith comes over and gives me first-hand supervision to make sure that I do what I'm supposed to do.

When I feel up to it, and sometimes even when I don't, I'll go down to the basement and just work out.

When the worst of winter arrives, in December or January, I head west, to California. The weather's much nicer out there then, and it's time to start working out seriously.

I get to see my mother and my brothers and sisters, and I train in a park that's in the neighborhood where I grew up. I've been going back there for more than nine years now.

I'm not the only player who goes home to

get ready for the season. I've got some buddies I meet every winter, and we work out together. Eric Davis and Chris Brown and a bunch of minor leaguers all show up at that same park. We do our exercises, we hit, we throw, we run. It's a big park, so we've got the opportunity to do just about anything we like to do.

I consider that time in the park as the workouts that get me conditioned, get me prepared for spring training and the new season.

When I work out at home, in my basement, I work on weights. Dumbbells, maybe 40-pound dumbbells. I'm not building muscle when I do that; I'm building for strength. I don't want to get bulky muscles. They make you slow and stiff, and that messes up your swing. It messes up your running, too.

I know that you hear about steroids in other sports, but I don't think they're widely used in baseball.

I ride my Lifecycle, my stationary bike, too. I may ride it 18 minutes a day. I don't know how many miles that comes to, because there are various levels at which you can ride, but I know that it's wonderful exercise for my legs.

Between all that and what I do in California, I feel that I'm ready when I head for spring training in Florida.

In '89, I came down a lot earlier than I had in any previous year. I was there even before the pitchers arrived, and I was working out and training on my own. The pitchers and the catchers usually get there earlier than the rest of us; their fundamentals are a lot harder than ours to go through.

Outfielders don't have too much to worry about. Making the right plays and throwing to the right bases, we can work that out in a couple of days. As we get closer to playing actual games in spring training, we get more into it all.

You try not to psyche yourself up too early in spring training. As a veteran ball player, I take it as it comes. I know the season's going to start, and I am excited about that, in my way, but at the same time I've got to be patient about it. I've got to remember that I have to pace myself. When you've got 162 ball games to play, and you do that for six months, you have to be prepared for the long year. You have to be in good shape and, just as important, in good spirits. That's what preparing yourself is really all about.

If you do it right, and you condition yourself during the course of the season as well, especially during the middle part of it, it helps you down the stretch.

You don't want your body to deteriorate. You don't want to get seriously tired. A lot of players understand that today, how important it is that you take care of yourself in mid-season, because that will benefit you during those hot days down the stretch.

I continue to do what I've done all along. I ride the cycle. I'm already active, doing a lot of running, but riding the cycle keeps me fit. And working with weights works, too, to keep my strength up. If you don't do stuff like that, your body will wear down in late August or September.

Of course, you've got to tend to your mind, too. Sometimes, spring training isn't so good for that.

Before I went to spring training in '89, I was doing some thinking about my relationship with the Mets. It was time to do that, I thought. After all, I've really played for only one team in my career. After a while, you are tempted to think of the team as your family. That's not such a big risk, of course, but you always have to remind yourself that baseball is a business. Sometimes things don't pan out the way you think they will.

That spring, I'd been with the same organization for nine years. Nine years of being in New York, of being with the Mets. When I got to spring training in '89, I had the '89 season and the following year remaining on my contract. The '90 year was my option year; the '89 season was guaranteed.

It's true that other guys were getting big salaries, but that wasn't my point. I probably deserve to be up there with those guys, but I wasn't griping about that. I was griping about the organization. I'd been with the Mets for a long time, and I had never griped over a contract negotiation. We never had one, anyway. I didn't want to have one then.

What I was trying to say to the ball club was, hey, just give me an extension from this point on. This year was guaranteed, just give me three more years to guarantee that I'll stay with the Mets and play with the Mets. That's what I wanted to stress. I wasn't saying that I wanted to get paid X because everybody else is getting paid that.

If that had been the issue, getting more money because other players were earning more than I was, I could have waited two years and become a free agent at 28. As a free agent, after two good seasons—and I was confident I'd have two good years—there would be a lot of clubs bidding for me.

I thought, I owe a lot to this organization and they owe a lot to me. It goes both ways.

I've been a member of the family for nine years, and there's no reason, after all that time, for me to have to sit here and tell them the only reason I want to renegotiate my contract is to get more money. That's not the issue.

But I have a lot of pride about playing for the Mets organization. And, don't forget, all my friends are here, too.

My agent, Eric Goldschmidt, put that on the table for the Mets to think about. At first, the Mets said we were asking for too much money. Well, Eric pointed out, how much did they think it was going to cost them next year if we had a big year in '89?

But Frank Cashen, who runs the team, is a very conservative man. I had the opportunity to speak with him, and told him what I thought about the organization, why I felt that I should be rewarded with a new contract. I told him, plainly, that I wanted to be a part of the Mets' organization for the remainder of my career. I didn't want to make a change. I told him that when stories came out about me wanting to play in L.A.—and they did come out during the playoffs in '88—people were making that a bigger issue than it was.

I told him that if I was in a situation where I was a free agent and I had the opportunity to play at home, why wouldn't I take it? It would be crazy of me to say that I wouldn't want to play at home. But the point I stressed to the Mets was that I didn't want the team to put me in that situation. Why should they take that chance, of losing a guy who's been with the organization for such a long time?

In the back of your mind, it's true that you do become aware of what other guys are getting. It just leaks out, through the press. I've had sportswriters come to me and tell me that they think I'm underpaid. A player who's had one good year gets a load of money. I've been a player who's had several good years and I've never griped about my contract before. In fact, I'm still not griping about it.

The organization told me we'd negotiate after the season. I was trying to get them to negotiate in the spring. Well, the way it developed, I finally thought I'd play through the '90 season, hit the free-agency market and see what happened.

At this point, there were—we're talking about spring training in '89—only two right fielders who were dominating players, putting up big numbers consistently—me and Jose Canseco. Andre Dawson has been a super player, but he's getting older. I'm going to be around a while and so is Canseco.

Whatever was going to happen, I remember thinking in spring training, I wasn't concerned about who was getting paid what. I was more concerned with getting paid for what I did. It's not a case of wanting to get paid such and such because Joe is getting such and such and he doesn't do what I do. I looked at it this way: every guy doesn't have my ability to do the things I do. I judge myself the way I perform once I put on that uniform and go on that field.

I am determined to be successful. I do play hard. I do not take it home with me, however. If I have bad days on the field, I live with those bad days. On the field, in the dugout, I'm the guy who shows his concern. I'm the one who's yelling and screaming in the dugout to get the team motivated.

Some people said that the idea to renegotiate came from my agent. It didn't. It came from me. I got to the point where I figured that if I wanted to continue to play in New York, and go through the abuse that I go through in the media, I might as well go ahead and get an extension on my contract.

If I didn't want to do that, I figured, hey, why don't I just play out the contract? What I was trying to show the Mets was that I had no problem with the media critics; I was so used to the media writing negative things about me that I used it to bring out the best in my performance. One sports announcer said that there was only one other player who thrived on that the way I have, and that was Reggie Jackson.

When he played in New York, the media would get on him, but he loved it. It made him work harder. It made him appreciate himself.

And that's how it's been with me. I don't get down on myself because of what they say. I tell myself, every time they say bad things about me, I'm just going to go out there and do better.

Well, all that came out in spring training, '89.

And I wasn't the only guy doing the talking. Keith Hernandez had his say, too.

During the time Keith and I were together on the team, we had some differences. Sure. There was a piece in *Esquire* about me, and Mike Lupica, who wrote it, had me saying that Hernandez really wasn't there for half a season.

I admitted to Hernandez that I said it, and he agreed that it was the truth. But I said it to Lupica in a nicer way than he wrote it.

Keith was really going through a tough time in those days, the time I was talking about. He was having personal problems with his marriage, and he wasn't really into what he had to do. I can appreciate that.

In spring training I was talking about my contract and my future with the Mets and the press was covering every word. One day I saw in the press that Hernandez—and Gary Carter, too, a guy I respect—was saying that I didn't need to be talking about that in spring training. Carter said that it wasn't the time to talk contract; we had come so close to winning in '88.

Most of the other players knew better. They said to themselves, it's not my business. It's Darryl's career. I'm not going to get involved in it. But Hernandez and Carter did get involved.

Then it was time to take the team picture. We were all on the field, getting ready. I saw Hernandez, and I told him, "Listen, you know I didn't get involved in your business about your negotiation on your contract, so why don't you just stay out of mine?"

Well, he said something back to me and I went after him.

No real damage was done.

A lot of people still don't understand my relationship with Keith. Keith had a lot on his mind when he was speaking out on my situation. He felt bad about it. We had to sit down and have a serious talk.

We did have a meeting with Dr. Alan Lans,

the team psychiatrist. He told me and Keith that we were crazy to let the press use us. You guys have been so close, he said, you've been helping each other for so many years. You shouldn't let the press destroy that friendship. He said that was what the press could do. They're out there laughing about it all; they get a big kick out of it.

He's a super guy, Dr. Lans. He's somebody you can talk to. Whatever's on your mind, you can tell him. He knows what goes on in the life of a professional ball player. And he gives advice; he makes you feel better. I know that a lot of the players have enjoyed talking with him: me, Doc, Hernandez. He's always available to us, even though he has his own practice in addition to working for the team.

That was how spring training began.

I felt better when I got to play.

I read somewhere that Whitey Herzog said that spring training goes on too long, that guys get hurt. I don't know if that's always been true, but I know that in '89, we had more games to play in spring training. They expanded the schedule and it was just entirely too long.

Down there, you're not really playing like it's the season. You're just sort of going through the motions, getting prepared, giving yourself an idea of what you want to do.

You get to a point where you know you're ready. Then, you start dragging during the last couple of weeks of spring training. By the end of it, you really want to get the season going.

The team's record, in itself, may not matter much in spring training. The best record in Florida may not lead to the best record during the season. That's because your regulars don't play the whole game in spring training. They play five, six, seven innings, and then you start looking at other players.

Spring training was useful in '89; it always is useful for me. But when I look back at that spring training in '89, Port. St. Lucie, Florida, wasn't such a happy place. There was that war of words about my contract. I walked out of camp for a day. A couple of hours after I came back, I hit a homer against the Dodgers.

I told the press that I came back "because I felt it's right for me to come back to be a part of this team and my teammates at this time."

They wanted to know what I'd do after the season.

"I'll play the year out and do what I have to do after that. I figure the ball club will pick up my option, but we discussed working

111

out a trade after this season. As for the future after that, I don't consider myself being a part of the New York Mets," I said.

But you can't sit around thinking about grievances. You're paid to play. I patched up my differences with Keith Hernandez, and when the team came north to start the season, I felt—for reasons that were important to me and to the team—that it was time to bear down. It was time for another season.

5

On the Field

Some players keep track of their stats. They always know where they are, how they're fielding, what they're hitting, how many stolen bases they have. I try to remember some of them, but I can't remember all of them, and when those baseball books come out every year, there's usually something in them that I didn't know about myself.

In '89, during the pre-season, I was told that my 186 homers, at age 27, were more than Reggie Jackson, Babe Ruth, Ted Williams and Willie McCovey had at my age. Hank Aaron and Willie Mays had more, which didn't surprise me.

I didn't know exactly what I was supposed

to feel about that stat, except that it made me proud. I guess I hoped I'd stay healthy during the rest of my career and climb up there with the leaders.

I use a 35-inch, 32-ounce bat, made by Adirondack. I don't even know what they cost; I think the club pays for them. It's not an endorsement. When I get a brand new bunch of bats, I look at them and see how tight the grain is. I may even give it a kiss and say nice things to it, so it treats me nice.

I use a bat with a wide barrel and a very narrow handle. I gave instructions to the people at Adirondack when they made the first bats for me. I like thin handles because they feel comfortable in my hands, and more weight in the barrel gives me more surface where I hit the ball. Some guys like to sand the handles of their bats; I don't have to because they're already the way I like them.

I use a Rawlings glove. It wasn't designed specifically for me, it already existed. I don't even remember whose model it was, but it's an open-faced glove; the webbing is open. I don't do anything special during the season to keep the glove in good condition. When I get a new glove, I have to break it in. You do that with balls, using the glove every day. I start the season with two new gloves, and I ask some of the pitchers on the club to break them in for me. Once the season starts, I can go through the entire season with just one glove. I like to use just one because I feel comfortable with the glove I've been using every day.

A friend showed me the entry about my '88 season in *The 1989 Elias Baseball Analyst*, a fat book filled with stats.

It read: "His 20 home runs against southpaws were the most by a lefty hitter against lefty pitchers since we started keeping such records in 1975. Out of curiosity, we went back and checked Maris in 1961 and Ruth in 1927: Maris had 12, Ruth 19...Has had 25+ homers and 25+ steals in each of last five years, tying major league record shared by Willie Mays (1956–60) and Bobby Bonds (1969–73)...Leads active players with one extra-base hit every 8.1 at-bats (minimum: 1000 PA)...Career home-run rate of one every 15.5 at-bats is 9th best in major league history (minimum: 150 HR)...Batting average with runners in scoring position, and average in Late-Inning Pressure Situations, were lowest of career."

Well, I guess you can't do everything well.

What's true for me is that I try to have confidence in myself and maintain my concentration about both the fundamentals and the subtleties of the game. The longer you play the game, the more you ought to be learning about how to play it.

Take fielding, for instance. You watch guys hit various pitchers, and you try to match up what you know the pitcher is doing with the batter's tendency against such pitches. If I'm in right field and the guy at bat isn't a power hitter, is more of a line drive hitter, I want to cut off the gaps. I don't play deep on him because I don't want him to line one between me and the center fielder. Of course, if you're out there and somebody like Galarraga or Will Clark or Andre Dawson is at bat, you've got to play back; you can play at an angle. It depends, too, on what pitcher is on the mound, so you have to know your own pitchers very well. Is that batter likely to catch up with Doc's best fast ball? And if he does, where will he be likely to hit it?

You might take a look at Doc when the game begins, and you say to yourself that he's throwing extremely hard, so you don't have to worry a lot about guys pulling the ball. You know the hitters are going to be late trying to hit Doc's fast ball. If it's a pitcher like Bobby Ojeda, okay, you know that most of the right-handed batters are going to be trying to hit the ball to right field, because Bobby throws a lot of change-ups. It's all a part of knowing the whole game. You know your pitchers and you know how they're pitching to particular batters. You play off your pitchers.

Of course, the outfielders share information about how to play certain guys. The center fielder is the captain of the outfield. You watch him carefully. If he moves, you move. If the center fielder moves over a little toward right, I move a little toward the line. I watch him.

I think about a game before I play it, about what situations might come up and what I'll have to do in them. I think that's why at this point in my career, I'm starting to really blossom into a player who knows what he can do.

When a guy comes up to the plate, I try to think about what he might do that will affect me. If he hits it here, I've got to do this. If he hits it there, I've got to do that. I try to be always prepared, a step ahead. I'm not saying that I'm always right, but given the odds, I'll be right the majority of the time.

When I'm on base, I pay attention to what's going on around me. To my coach at first and my coach at third. To the pitcher and the catcher and the batter.

Once the game starts, I'm into it. When I get to first, I talk to the coach. I will tell him that if the batter hits a double, I'll go all the way home. My mind is made up.

I'm on first. The ball is hit. I see it's going in the alley. I'm scoring. That's how it goes. What you have to do as a base runner is to prepare yourself before anything even happens. You have to know what you're going to do.

We've all seen the third base coach stop guys who are racing toward third on their way home. They don't stop me. I've already got it. I know I can make it. Once I know the ball is clear, I'm off. There's no stopping me. That's part of my game. It's part of my personality.

It's true what you've heard about stealing; you steal off the pitcher, not the catcher. You get the jump off the pitcher and that jump means a lot. The catcher has nothing to do with it. All he can do is throw the ball, and even if he has a great arm, he can't make up for what the pitcher gave you.

If the pitcher takes too long, you can make it. There are many power pitchers in the league, and power pitchers are real slow to the plate. Their techniques make them great pitchers. But even Nolan Ryan, a great pitcher, is slow to the plate.

He's got a high kick, great form, and that's what gives him something extra on the pitch. But you can steal on that windup. A guy who's not a power pitcher, on the other hand, is going to be quicker to the plate, because he doesn't have to go through that long motion.

A lot of pitchers are changing their motions now, because they got tired of having guys steal on them all the time. That attitude can screw up your whole game, though. When you spend your time on the mound worrying about whether or not a guy is going to steal, you're not thinking about the hitter.

Doc Gooden, however, has told me that they can steal all the bases they want off of him. The guy at the plate still has to hit the ball. The best stealing can do, he thinks, is get a guy to third. The guy at bat is the one Doc worries about.

I'm proud of my hitting. A lot of fans know I can field and I can run, but they know me best as a hitter.

Some hitters go up there and guess what the pitcher is going to throw. You might get that pitch and you might not. It's that old line again: if you hit it safely three times out of ten, you're a great hitter.

That also means that seven out of ten times, the pitcher has the edge on you.

That's why I don't play the guessing game. I want to see the pitch and know what it is.

Zones are the way hitters divide up the strike zone. You are looking for a certain

121

pitch at a certain time. It changes from pitch to pitch, according to the situation you're in. At the most there are three zones for me. I select one and figure the pitch will be in it. If I'm right, maybe I'll make contact, or better, maybe I'll hit it solidly where no one can catch it. If I'm wrong, maybe I'll miss the pitch or just let it go.

I've got a split second to react. There's no other way you can react. Fast. You see it; you hit it.

Say there are runners on first and second, and the count on me is 2–2. I figure the pitcher isn't going to give me a fast ball to hit. I'm waiting for something off-speed. I'm locked in: if he does give me a fast ball, I'm going to crush it. If he doesn't give me a fast ball, I'm going to take it. Of course, if it's a mistake, a breaking ball that he hangs, I'm going to crush that, too. Your mind has to be locked in to what you're going to do whatever the situation.

That's not guessing. When you're guessing, you're up there and the pitcher's in his motion, and all of a sudden you don't know what's coming. He throws one away—and you didn't guess away—and you wind up swinging on a bad pitch.

If you're looking for a pitch in a certain zone, you're not guessing. If the pitch is in your zone, instead of in some other zone, you swing at it. You were looking for it. If it's not there, I try not to swing.

Actually, I may be looking at more than one area. I may be looking at two or three different zones.

I always know the count; that's elementary. It's the clue to what the pitcher may try to do. How many runners are on? How many runs are you up or down? Is it early in the ball game?

A good pitcher won't tip off the pitch by his delivery. You can't tell what it is until it comes out of his hand, so you want to see the ball come out. When I see the ball leave the pitcher's hand, I can see whether it's straight or if there's a spin on it.

I've got a split second to figure it out. It's a blessing to have that talent. If you know the pitch, you can hit it. Maybe. Sometimes I think about that and I realize how incredible it is. People don't realize what it's like to hit a ball that's coming at you so hard. The pitcher always has the advantage.

He has another advantage. He can throw it at you. And hit you.

I've heard people say that throwing at batters is just part of the game. That's like saying if I hit a home run off a pitcher, that's part of the game, too. But it's not the same thing. When a pitcher strikes me out, he feels good. When I hit a homer, I feel good. But what good does it do to hit a batter? I don't understand that.

Guys say that throwing at guys, brushing people off the plate, all that, is something you should get used to. Not a chance. You can kill somebody with a baseball.

I think they ought to change the rules. If a pitcher throws at you and hits you intentionally, he ought to be tossed out of the game. Right then.

And believe me, it's no mystery if a guy is throwing intentionally.

When a pitcher hits you, a pitcher who's been around a long time and who doesn't have control problems, you know. You can see the pitcher's arm. You know when he's not aiming at the catcher's glove. The catcher's glove is there. Your body is there. He's aiming at you. There's no such thing as a pitch getting away when a pitcher throws it right at you.

Once I got hit in the head. On the helmet, thank God, and fortunately it had a flap. Mike Mason was pitching for Chicago; he was a left-handed pitcher. It was in '87, at Shea, and I'd faced him in the minors; he always had a lot of control problems. That was one case where I don't think he wanted to hit me. But I was out on the ground. My head was spinning; I didn't know what anybody was saying to me. It was scary. I'd rather not have it happen again. Guys have done it to me since then, but I always let them know how I felt about it.

Mike Mason sent me a telegram the next day apologizing for what he did, saying he didn't mean to hit me.

That was a classy act.

I guess getting hit is one of the dangers of being a home run hitter. But the truth is I don't usually go up to the plate saying to myself that I want to hit a home run. I just say that I want to hit my pitch. There's no point in going up to bat thinking about hitting a homer. Just go up there, concentrate, have confidence, hit the ball hard.

When you're hitting, it's important to be relaxed. I don't play head games with myself before I go to bat. I don't sit in the dugout and think, what is Sutcliffe going to throw to me today? Once you start doing that, you confuse your mind. All you have to do is play the game the proper way, as a professional, and you'll be successful.

I know that some guys in this game—managers, pitchers, a few hitters—use computers. That's not the real thing. The real thing is the guy out there with the ball in his hand. I couldn't really sit down and look at a computer and say, well, I haven't had success against that guy and then figure out what to do at the plate. If I start thinking like that, I'm going to put myself in the hole before I hit. I'm beat before I bat.

I don't need a computer to hit the ball.

I hit a long home run in Yankee Stadium when we played the Yankees just before the regular season began in '89. Somebody told me that it was the longest one he'd ever seen there. Bill Robinson, our coach, said that someday I would hit a ball farther than anybody has ever hit one.

Well, I don't even think about that. I don't remember all the homers I've hit, even the long ones. Once you become a home run hitter, you get to the point where you don't think about it. As long as it clears the fence, it's a home run. They're all the same to me.

There are some stats, I'm told, that indicate that I hit better on artificial turf. That's not so surprising. I hit balls on a line and they fly on that turf. You get them in the gap quickly and they really carry. It's different from playing on grass.

I hit better on the road in '88 than I did at home. Maybe it's the motivation involved. The fans boo you, and you want to do well when that happens. It's normal for them to boo you, so you just get through it and do what you have to do. It doesn't bother me at all.

Left-handed pitchers don't give me much trouble, either. That was one improvement I made after coming up to the majors. I realized that I had to do it if I was going to move to another level of skill. I had to tell myself that I wasn't going to be intimidated by lefties. I was going to learn to hit them, to be selective and get the pitch that I wanted.

Building confidence has been crucial in my career. I remember that I had a bad spell in August, 1988, but that wasn't because I lost faith in myself. It was a long summer, a very hot summer. Everywhere we went, everywhere we played, it was hot. I played two months straight without a day off, because Hernandez was hurt that summer and Davey just couldn't afford to take me out of the lineup.

I've been working on my stamina ever since. I don't want to have another hot August do me in the way that one did.

During spring training in '89, I told a local sports reporter in Florida that "last year was like an average season, because I got burned out in August. This is going to be a monster season."

I want to feel good about the season before it starts. I want to win it all. "I don't think we have to win it," I told Dave Anderson of the *New York Times* when the '89 season started. "But I think we should." It's the goal that all of the veterans on the team can appreciate. The Dodgers got there ahead of us in '88. We didn't forget that.

Before the '89 season, I told a reporter, "We're sure of ourselves. We know we're good, we know we can turn it on and we do. But it's not the best way to handle a season, and it's absolutely not the way to handle a playoff."

Doc told that same reporter, "The only way to handle a season is to go out and win from Opening Day. Play .600 ball for six months. I know it's a long season and it's hard to stay at that level. But it's too dangerous to lie low for a while and then crank things up in the homestretch. I don't know why we do it that way. I guess we're just that sure of ourselves."

It's all a matter of attitude, which may be as important as hitting homers and running bases and covering the outfield.

When the '89 season finally began, we opened at home against the Cardinals. The first game may not mean more than one game, but I like to think it's a clue to the way the season could go. Doc pitched and won, 8–4, striking out eight. I got two doubles and a single and stole two bases. I was 3–3 with two RBIs.

It felt good. I didn't know then, of course, how the year would go after that.

Pressures
and Pleasures

Most of the year you're out there on the field, playing ball. But when you're not—and that means after games, before games, during the off-season—your mind is filled with things to worry about and things to appreciate. A baseball player who makes more money than the average working guy has to take care of business off the field too.

I really try to avoid thinking about money. I know that it's a blessing that I have the opportunity to make so much money and take care of the people who are important to me. But that's not the biggest thing in life.

I get good advice about my money from my agent. But I have my own mind. I've been in the business for such a long time that I know how to manage money.

At one time, I didn't know all that. You learn by going through it, by letting someone else decide how to save your money and how to spend it, the way my first agent did. I let him handle everything, without checking on what he was doing, because I put my trust in people. But when you get older you get wiser, too, and you want to be a factor in your own investments. You sit down one day, and you analyze your situation, and you think, hey, I'm the one who's out there making all the money, so I'm going to start keeping track of where it's all going. I want to decide how to put dollars aside for my kids' future.

You have to use your head in this business. A lot of people who watch me play, they think, well, all he has to do is go out there and hit the ball and put the money in a bank. It's not that easy. I try to keep in mind that there's a life for me after baseball.

When the Mets put out a paycheck, they send it directly to me. I get that check in my hand every payday. Nobody else receives that check unless I send it to them. Some athletes have their money sent to some guy who invests it for them. I guess that's all right if you trust the guy and he's proved to you that he knows what he's doing.

When I was a kid, I didn't know anything about money. We didn't have a lot of it. My father worked, and later, my mother worked, too. We weren't starving, but we weren't rich, either. You grow up and you don't really know about big money until you find yourself involved in it. And when you do get involved in it, if you put it in other people's hands you won't know what's happening to it; you won't learn how to handle it.

As your mind grows to keep up with your body, you have to start paying attention. When you're a professional athlete and you're young, they just throw money at you right away, and you may not pay any attention to it. But if you start growing into your own self, one thing you learn is the value of a dollar. Once you start realizing that, you start learning how to budget money. You make plans and programs for yourself and your family that will benefit everybody after your career's over.

You have to figure that out on your own, no one else can figure it out for you. There are a lot of people out there who would love to, but you're the one who's making the money, so you have to use your own head. There comes a point in your life when you have to sit down and look at things. You have to see where you've been and where you want to be down the road.

Of course, I know I'm not an investment expert, so I put a lot of my money right into the bank. Later, if I find something I want to invest in, I can decide. But for me, the best thing is an investment in money. And property. That can be profitable, too.

People wonder, well, after you spend some and save some, what do you do with what's left? I put it in my kids' names. That's the greatest investment of all. I can give them something I didn't have when I was a kid. Trust funds in their names.

Say one day some guy comes to me, a guy I know, and he wants me to put some money in a new mall somewhere. I'll decide. I won't necessarily call anyone about it before I do that. If I want some advice, though, my agent, who's also an accountant, will let me know if it's a legitimate investment. I don't forget that there are a lot of crooks out there along with the good people.

Your agent has to be honest. If he really cares about you, he won't take advantage of you. He's there in your corner all the time. If you realize he's not there for you, it's time to make a change.

Look at boxing. To me, it doesn't seem like a clean profession. It's all for money. They rip you off without a thought. I think there's only one guy who's not getting ripped off in boxing, because he's very smart, and that's Sugar Ray Leonard. He knows what he's doing. He's clean, a good fighter, a great fighter, and the man is smart.

In my life, I don't want to get ripped off. So I work with people I trust. That's easy.

I've got a company called Darryl Strawberry Pro Sports. It handles all the promotional work I do. The William Morris Agency represents me, as well, and it works with Darryl Strawberry Pro Sports.

So far, my major endorsements have been with Rawlings and Nike. But there'll be more. I've been talking to AT&T about running some baseball clinics for kids, with me as the spokesman. I've done some TV commercials, too, including one for a milk company and one for a brand of yogurt.

I guess you'd have to say that I haven't done a lot of that kind of stuff yet, but I am planning to get more involved in it. I want my little company to have its own income. When I do a card show—one of those events where I show up to sign autographs and people pay to get in and I get a portion of what is taken in—I send the money to Darryl Strawberry Pro Sports. That's a beginning.

I can trust the staff of Darryl Strawberry

Pro Sports. My mother, Ruby, is the president. She's been working for my career since she retired from the phone company in late '85. My sister Michelle is the executive vice president and my sister Regina is the corporate secretary. My brother Ronnie is the PR director. My brother Michael, who was once in the Dodger organization, is now in the Los Angeles police department or he'd probably be working alongside the others.

Money isn't the only factor in a player's life, however.

It seems to me we're in a time when there are more temptations than ever. A lot of ball players make more money than they ever dreamed of seeing when they were younger. They don't know what to do with it.

I don't feel weak when I'm faced with temptation. You really have to get to know yourself in this life. It takes a while, sure, for you to get wiser about a lot of things. I think a lot of the young guys in baseball have trouble with the pressure. Even worse than the pressure is the fact that they haven't yet learned to be happy with themselves, *in* themselves. Once you start being satisfied with who you are, there is no pressure. It's all a head game, you know.

You're doing this because the Lord has blessed you with the ability to play the game.

That's something I say all the time. But if you start thinking that baseball is a pressure game, that's when you start confusing yourself and get involved in things you otherwise wouldn't get involved in.

When you hang around a while, you see the kind of damage that guys can do to themselves, with drugs, with drink. The best way to avoid getting into trouble is to stay at home. Simple enough? I'm not saying that you have to stay at home all the time; that would be ridiculous. But I've got a job and I have responsibilities to take care of. Once you know that, you start feeling different about those temptations.

The best advice is to know yourself. That's helpful when you're dealing with women, too.

In the minors, wherever I went, there were girls around. They've always been around ball players. They always will be.

Some of them want to get involved, really involved, with a ball player. They want to get married and settle down. But I think that what often goes through their minds is that they see a ball player they think is handsome, unique. And they say to themselves that he's trying to do something for himself that will make his life better. Guys who aren't ball players may not be as appealing to those girls. Those guys, the girls think, are just out for one thing, having an affair, and they don't want to be tied down and get married.

Ball players want to get married. The safest way to keep out of trouble these days is to get married.

If you're very successful, a well-known player, and you don't have a steady woman that you're seeing, you have to be very nervous about all sorts of things that can happen. Diseases, of course. But also, there are young ladies out there who want to grab for the big dollars. They know that you've got a household name. A girl could have an affair with you, then sell her story to a magazine for thousands of dollars.

Look at Wade Boggs. The woman in that case met Boggs, and he was very successful, and they had a long affair. But he was married, and he wanted to break off the affair. The woman didn't want to let him walk after she'd put so much time into it.

Sometimes you have an affair with a woman, and you start telling her everything about yourself. That's really asking for trouble.

And then there are those players who don't seem to care what happens. They're out there with their big eyes, looking for any cooperative woman. Young guys are like that, because that's where their minds are at: having a great time; being a ball player; enjoying all the women you possibly can. They don't understand that when they start making the big money, they have to be careful about getting involved because some women want to take you straight to the bank.

I guess I'm too romantic for that.

I met Lisa at the L.A. Forum, at a Lakers' game. I met her through a friend of mine who introduced us. I saw her and said, "Oh my God, look at that beautiful girl over there." That was after my rookie season in 1983. I was really turned on by her. We got together, and I visited her a couple of times and sent her flowers. I was the real gentleman.

When it comes right down to it, when you feel really good about someone and you start liking someone, you do things that come naturally to you.

She was a very happy person, a beautiful one.

After we got married, I discovered that it wasn't so easy. Lisa saw the lifestyle of a baseball player; because I was famous, girls would be around trying to get her man. Women would come up to me even when we were out to dinner together. If a girl tried to get close and wanted to put her hands on me, Lisa might say something.

We were married in 1985 and had our troubles not so long after that. We had one child, Darryl, Jr.

Maybe the wildness in me was a factor. A major league player, traveling all over the country, hanging out a lot, drinking and getting into stuff that I shouldn't have gotten into. I can tell the truth about it, because it happens to the best of us. But there comes a time when you find yourself and decide to change your life.

Well, Lisa moved out on me and went back to California. One of the sportswriters in New York wrote a nasty article. He said that Lisa left me and the Mets should get rid of me and that I was no good—or something like that. I went down to Florida, to spring training, and I saw that writer. I told him that I would destroy him if he ever did that again. He was very nervous. I haven't talked to him, really, since then.

Lisa and I did get back together; I think it was never really over. We were apart most of the year of '87 and got back together that September. I think we realized we cared about each other and had a son to care about. We didn't want to walk our separate ways; we felt that we could make it.

During that year when we were apart I talked to her a lot. I would call her because

I wanted to talk to my son. When I'd go to the west coast I'd see Darryl, Jr., and Lisa and I started seeing each other again.

Of course, I was going out with other women at the time. I wasn't going to sit around and wait. I'm quite sure she wasn't sitting around and waiting, either.

It was a lesson we had to learn. Did she want to be out there with other guys, did I want to be out there with other girls, or did we want to make a family? We decided to try again.

Then, Diamond Nicole arrived, a beautiful little girl. I was living alone, in New York. Lisa had moved back to California. But even with two kids to love, it wasn't right. I never did make a list of what went wrong. I guess that's what you pay lawyers to do.

Through it all, I often thought about how I wanted to be a good and loving father to the kids. Lisa would tell me how hard it was for her to take care of the kids when I was away. I didn't want to hear that, really. But I wanted to be a good father. I want my kids to grow up and recognize their father as someone who made them appreciate life. I want to teach them how you go out there into the world and approach people and present yourself so they will accept you. I don't want my kids to try to be anything that they can't be. Just be yourself is my message to them. You have to keep an eye on your kids and make sure that they're going in directions that will benefit them throughout their lives.

Sometimes the pressure of a bad marriage can build up inside you. You sit down at home alone, with yourself, and those tears come.

I finally figured out that there were going to be problems between me and my wife. When I figured that out, and knew that we would have to get a divorce, it really hurt. It's not all her fault and it's not all my fault, but things really didn't work out the way I thought they would. Two people can love each other, and still not be able to be together. Knowing that hurt me, because we had two beautiful kids.

My kids are my life. That's who I go out there and play baseball for—my son and my daughter. Sure, I'm playing because of the pride in being a professional athlete and the pride in being a Met. But it's important to me to achieve something that my kids can appreciate.

As far as the marriage is concerned, Lisa sued for divorce, after four years of marriage, in '89. A reporter interviewed me, and I told him that there were no hard feelings on my part, that I thought it would be best to get out of the marriage, get on with my life and let her get on with hers.

That was easy to say. Meanwhile, I'm supposed to be playing ball.

That kind of thing is tough on you. You think about your kids a lot. I think about the fact that they're out there in California and I'm in New York. I hope that they're around good people; that's my concern. If anything happened to my babies, I'd kill for them.

I've always said that just because things don't work out between two people, two adults, it doesn't mean that the kids should suffer. They have nothing to do with what went wrong with the adults. If Lisa isn't able to take care of the kids by herself, then I'll be happy to take them. I'll have my family or somebody I trust come and stay with me and care for them. I have to travel; that's my life. But I will take care of my kids.

I had to get out of that marriage while I had a chance, while there was still plenty of time left in my career. It's no good for a person to sit around being unhappy. When I'm out there busting my tail to play ball and do my best, and at the same time, I'm unhappy with the woman I'm living with, it's not a good situation. You play head games with yourself and you really can't concentrate.

I guess, looking back, that it was just a bad

experience. We really loved and cared for each other once, but it got to a point where we just couldn't be with each other anymore. I don't think she handled my success as well as she should have. She wasn't able to be really supportive of me. I guess she wanted more out of life than watching me succeed.

I don't exactly know what she did want. She might have wanted me around more often than I was. But there was nothing I could do about that, and she knew that when she married me. My lifestyle wasn't a strange one—traveling, being away, playing ball— that's all. Fortunately, I could afford to get a divorce.

What's strange is that whenever this kind of thing happens to me, I think it's all very private. Then I pick up a paper and there it is. The job is tough enough to do without adding any outside frustration to it.

One story mentioned that I resented my own father for leaving home when I was just 13. Would my kids resent me?

"It will *not* happen," I told that reporter. "My kids will know that I care for them. I'll always be there for them. You don't neglect kids. The thing to do is to love them and to cherish them."

Friends help. Doc has helped, by listening to me. He's supportive. Bill Robinson, the coach, told the reporter, "I'm not too macho to give him a hug if I think he needs it. You have to deal with it. I feel he can do it."

I remembered when Keith Hernandez went through his divorce. It was long and angry. The game was his salvation. "For me," he said, "it was a relief. You are playing a game. That was the easy part for me. It would have been worse if I had not been playing."

I'm not sure I'm that strong. But I know that life goes on, no matter what happens.

Divorce is the worst kind of pressure. But there are others, if you're an athlete in New York.

I've heard for years that the New York press is the worst in the country. In other cities, the press wants to build you up if you've got talent. In New York, they want to tear you down. I've fought for my own survival in New York, just to keep my head above water. Here, the press wants to know everything you do, day and night, whether you're playing or in private.

It's always seemed to me that your personal life is none of their business. A sportswriter is supposed to write about sports. In other words, they should write about your performance on the field. But they ask you about other players, ask you to help them invade a teammate's privacy. I try to be honest when I'm asked a question, and if it hasn't anything to do with me, or how I play the game, I just say that has nothing to do with Darryl Strawberry.

I'm not anti-media. There are a lot of sportscasters on TV and radio (and some guys in print, too) who have a great knowledge of the game. They know what it takes for a player to perform. They have to do their jobs, to describe the game and how it's played, but they try to get listeners, viewers, to understand how tough it is to do well consistently. Players are on such a high pedestal that when they don't achieve, it's easy to say they're no good. Usually, that's not true. The best sportscasters understand what a guy has to live up to.

Vin Scully is one who knows the game well. He's been around a long time. Tim McCarver. He knows it all, as a player and as a broadcaster. Tom Seaver, I know him; he played the game and he played it very well.

Writers can be another matter. Playing in New York, especially. I'm out on the field trying to accomplish something for myself, not for the writers. The writers tend to make a big story out of nothing. That's the bottom line. And I say what I think. On the team bus, one of our guys said to me, "You're just like E. F. Hutton. Anything you say, they're going to listen to and make a big thing out of."

There are good reporters and bad ones. Joe Durso of the *New York Times* never invades anybody's privacy. But if one of the other writers asks if a certain guy has a drug problem, I just tell him, hey, that's not my business. But they never stop trying to get a story that will hurt some player or make public something that ought to stay private.

But being in New York means being on the Mets, for me, and that's good news, as far as playing with the guys on the team is concerned.

We're veteran ball players, and that means we're more relaxed about what we have to do. All we have to do is go out there and perform. Once you reach that point in your career where you have that experience underneath your belt, there's no reason for you to sit around talking. When you first start at the major league level, it's good to see every pitcher and talk about the little things. A lot of young players today don't talk enough about the game.

I've had conversations with several young players. Sometimes, the young guys go through a real tough time, and I try to keep their motivation going. I always tell them, one thing you can't do is get down on yourself.

Once that happens, you've beaten yourself before you get into the batter's box. There's enough pressure in the majors without adding to it.

In '88, at the end of the season, the press was building up Gregg Jefferies. The organization didn't want to rush him; they thought he was ready to play at this level and he was; he had all the talent. But the media made him the next Rookie of the Year.

That makes it hard for a young player. If you don't get off to a real good start—and for Jefferies that meant in '89—it's tougher on you.

It's important to think about winning, of course. Joe Magrane, the pitcher for the Cardinals, said something about the '87 series that the Cardinals played against the Minnesota Twins. He was saying that he didn't do well in that series and that he realized his "mentality was, dear God, don't let me screw up, instead of I'm gonna whip your ass."

There's a big difference. The best thing is to go out there and let your natural ability take over. Don't worry. Don't think about it. Just play. When you think about screwing up at the plate, all of a sudden you're 0–2.

On the Mets, we help each other do our best. We rarely put down our teammates.

I'm the type of person who doesn't dislike

anybody. I don't like to go around saying negative things. When I say things that may hurt someone, I do it because it's the truth.

I've had guys stab me in the back a few times.

One did it by talking to the press and saying that if he was voting for MVP, he really shouldn't vote for me. He should vote for McReynolds.

That's just how it is, sometimes—jealousy. I was having a super year and I was getting a lot of recognition. I was carrying the club for two months almost by myself because nobody was hitting. I guess the player, who I won't name, felt insecure about himself and felt bad he wasn't playing as well as I was.

You try to control your anger. I don't get pissed in public. After all, we're supposed to be a family.

We've got some real classy pitchers. Once in a while someone in the field will make an error, and it will cost the pitcher three or four runs. I remember one time when Darling was pitching. I messed up and caused a couple of runs. I misplayed a ball. I told Darling that I should have had it. He said, "Dude, don't worry about it, man, because you win so many ball games for me when I'm out there, I can't worry about one mistake that you make."

That's the kind of guys we have on the team. Our pitchers don't stare at you when you make a mistake, look you up and down and let the world know that they're pissed. They just get the ball and go back on the mound and do their thing. They never say anything about it.

We've got a great group.

I think that's very special to the Mets. We play to win. That's not true of all other teams. Other teams have players who are jealous of each other, because one guy's making more money than the next guy. In New York, the press tries to make us sound like that, but we're not. We're different.

Totally different from the Yankees. Their franchise is built around older players. Our franchise is built around younger ones. We have kids, compared to them, guys like Jefferies, myself, Gooden, Darling, Cone. Young players stick together. They don't pull apart and go separate ways.

The Yankees have a lot of ego trips going on—about who's getting all the money and who's getting the publicity and who's going to write the next book. We don't have that and we don't worry about that.

We can talk about each other on the bus and have a great time, because it's not mean stuff. It's just playful. Stay happy and keep winning.

When we screwed up, Davey Johnson didn't really say much. He may have said something simple: you've got to cut down on making mental mistakes. And when he said it, it was true. He wouldn't call you in and chew you out.

A lot of teams aren't together. Nine guys go out to play, but deep down inside they all go their separate ways. If you want to be a winning club, you've got to stick together. We do that. On the road, we find things to do together.

For the record, some of the guys on the Mets do have nicknames. David Cone is Conehead. We used to call Ron Darling "Mister Perfect," but now we just call him Ronnie. Sid Fernandez is El Sid. Dwight Gooden used to be Doc, but lately he's Uptown. Bob Ojeda is Bobby O. Barry Lyons is Mattresshead. Mackey Sasser is Sassy. Kevin Elster is Ellie. We call Greg Jefferies Ty Cobb. Howard Johnson is Hojo and, also, Hadji Shiek. Dave Magadan is called Magsie. And Keith Miller is Rex. Tim Teufel is Richard. Kevin McReynolds is Big Mac. And most guys call me Straw.

We don't sit around talking about baseball in our free time, because we know what we have to do on the field. Many of us have grown together into this Mets team.

Even the new guys—Cone, for one—have joined in with the bunch. Our team is unique because we do so many things together. No guy on the Mets has to be lonely. When a guy wants to go out, five or six others will go along with him.

When you're down, the others pick you up. "Come on, man, let's go out, let's have a good time. Forget about *that*. Let's not even think about it."

There's no pressure in being a Met.

It's a pleasure to travel with the team, too. For me, the most comfortable ball parks are on the west coast, in San Diego and in Los Angeles. They're beautiful parks, good to hit in. And the atmosphere out there is real laid back, relaxing. The fans aren't crazy, either.

When you're on the road, what you really look for is a nice quiet dinner. In some cities, you can't go out because there are too many people who want to make a name for themselves, stir up stuff, try to get you into a fight.

I don't worry about it. I walk away from people like that. I know how people are, so when they have something smart to say, I just go on about my business. I don't stoop to their level.

When I can get some peace and quiet, I find

a fine steak house—there are plenty of them on the east coast—and eat the kind of food I really like. I like Mexican food, too, and there's plenty of that on the west coast.

That's fun for me, to have a good meal with a bunch of teammates.

In fact, I guess just playing baseball is fun for me. That's number one. The major problem with the game today, what takes the fun out of it, is the way the press makes up stuff, puts labels on players, lays pressure on players to achieve more than they're capable of achieving when they're young. That's what takes the fun out of it for the young kid.

But for me, it's all still fun.

7

1989:
Getting Down
to Business

In spring training, we had reasons to be optimistic. We'd won our division in '88 and come close to winning the league title. I know that close doesn't count, but we were determined in '89 to make up for that lost chance.

No team had a better pitching staff: Doc, Darling, Cone, Fernandez and Ojeda to start, and Aguilera, Leach, Myers and McDowell to relieve.

We had our team leaders: Carter, Hernandez and me.

We had solid catching, an infield manned by Elster, Hernandez, Jefferies, Hojo, Tim Teufel and Dave Magadan.

Kevin McReynolds was in left. Lenny

Dykstra and Mookie Wilson could split center, and I was in right.

After our opening day, at Shea, when we beat St. Louis, 8–4, I felt good. My three hits and two RBIs were, I hoped, a sign of good things ahead. Doc went seven innings, struck out eight, gave up just five hits. And Don Aase, a nonroster player in spring training, made the team and turned in two good innings in relief of Doc. Jefferies had two hits, and Hojo and Elster had three each.

It looked like we were off to a good start.

Two weeks later, everything had changed. We lost six out of eight. We were in last place, with a record of 3–7. Davey Johnson issued a warning to cut out playing golf and cards and "lackluster" baseball and to start living up to our "billings."

"If I'm going to take the heat, I'm going to pass it down," Davey said to the press. "This is a very capable team," he said. "I don't believe it's been overestimated. It has lots of 'gamers' and lots of pride. But the only way you get your billing is to give great performances all the time. This is a serious business, and we all get paid very well to do what we're doing."

On April 16, against the Cardinals, I hit two homers, but we lost 5–3.

When the press asked me what was going

on, I told them: "We really stink. It's not a pleasant moment around this club. We have to work for it. We can't go through the motions anymore."

But I wasn't playing well and I knew it.

It was a rough time for the whole club. I wasn't being patient enough at the plate. I was trying to do it with one swing all the time. Bill Robinson and I had a long talk, and he told me I'd have to go back to the basics, just hitting the ball hard. I wanted to make things happen for me and hoped that would affect the others. I went back to doing the things I can do; I started using the whole field again. All of a sudden, it started to come back to me.

When I said that we were really stinking, I meant it. We were going through the motions and we might score runs early in the game, but then the other team would score some and we'd just sit there.

What happens is that guys get off to a rough start and then they start reading the papers too much. We have pride, and when you open the paper and see what's being written, it just eats you up. I tell the younger players not to read the papers.

By late in April we'd had a two-game winning streak. Not much, but something. Then the Cubs with Rick Sutcliffe beat Ojeda,

8–4. Ojeda had pitched four times and had lasted just over 18 innings, giving up 30 hits and 18 earned runs. It was not promising for such a good guy and such a good pitcher.

Even worse, for me, was getting hurt. It was against the Phillies. Steve Ontiveros was pitching. He threw me a change-up, and it was a cold night, and I swung too hard at it. I was way out in front of it.

Actually, I hit the pitch. I grounded out to the first baseman. But when you swing hard like that and it's cold out, you can get the most important part of your body out too much. I got my right shoulder out and I pulled something. The team's surgeon, Dr. Parkes, said that a few fibers were torn, a tendon was strained. I had to rest for a couple of days. There was pain involved and the medication I took made me groggy.

I came back to play against the Cubs, but my shoulder was hurting. I had to miss five games.

At the end of April, we had a six-game winning streak and were in Houston for a series with the Astros. Mike Scott pitched against us. We'd had good luck against him. In fact, he hadn't beaten us since May 1985. But he was ready. He had to leave the game with a tight left hamstring, but he won it, 7–6, making his record 4–1. David Cone lasted just two-and-a-third innings. We had the tying run on base in the ninth, and I was up. Dave Smith was in relief for Houston. Up to that moment, I had two hits, an RBI and my fifth home run. But I didn't get it done. I grounded out.

It made me think. Smith isn't an overpowering pitcher. He's a finesse pitcher. He tries to keep the ball down in the strike zone. He tries to get you to hit the ground ball. I've been up against him often, but I usually wind up walking.

What happened then was that I chased his pitch. I was overanxious in that situation—ninth inning, tying run on. I wasn't as disciplined as I know I can be. I should have waited for a pitch that I could really drive.

But there were plenty of games left in the season.

When May arrived I was hitting .288, but I hadn't really gotten into gear yet. I was striking out more times than I thought I should.

I think it had something to do with my shoulder. I had come back from that, of course, but I think I was trying too hard and I was a little rusty after the layoff. You get back in the lineup and want to do more than you're able to do. I was overswinging, not staying on the ball. I started off the season well, was in a good groove, then all of a sudden I got hurt. It takes you out of your whole game. You have to get it back slowly. There was a time when I couldn't do anything the right way. But I began to come back.

Early in May, Bobby Ojeda beat the Braves 7–1 in Atlanta. That was a good sign. It was the first win for Bobby since he'd severed the finger on his pitching hand the previous September. That kept us on our streak; we had won eight out of nine by May 2. I hit my sixth homer, on a 3–2 pitch, with Hojo on second, from Pete Smith.

Smith is a hard thrower, a good fast ball and a good breaking ball. But he's a young pitcher, and he made a mistake with me. He tried to sneak a good fast ball by me. He didn't think I could get around on it.

By May 4, we were tied for the division lead with the Cardinals and the Expos, with the Cubs just a half game out.

That week, we lost to the Reds 6–4 at Shea. Jose Rijo gave us four runs and nine hits in six innings and struck out six. Rob Dibble and John Franco cleaned up. I had three hits, an RBI, and an inside-the-park homer. Kal Daniels misjudged the ball, then made a wild throw. It was the second time I'd had an inside-the-park homer. And it was my seventh homer of the season.

Getting an inside-the-park homer isn't easy. It takes just the right kind of play. You hit a deep fly and it hits off the wall and the outfielder tries to make the play, but the ball bounces away from him, into the field. Sometimes the outfielder bangs against the wall, goes one way while the ball goes another. The rest is up to me and the third base coach. As I'm running, I keep watching the play develop. Then, as I come into third, I pick up the coach and if he's waving me on or stopping me, I have to make a decision.

As we moved along in May, we lost a little bit of momentum. My batting average started to fall. On May 7, the Astros beat Doc at Shea, 5–0. It was Doc's first loss of the year and made him 5–1. Kevin Bass went crazy against us that day, with 3-for-3 and four stolen bases. Jim Deshaies got the shutout. Doc lasted just six innings, his shortest outing of the season.

That week, Jose Rijo beat us again, 3–0. The Reds stole five bases. Rijo gave up just two hits in seven innings; I got one of those, a single. Bobby Ojeda lost again.

Losing to Rijo isn't exactly a shock. He's a good pitcher, with a good fast ball and a good breaking ball. And he seems to pitch well against us.

But we didn't sit around and moan. We're

pros. The next time we face him, we thought, we have to remember how he pitched to each of us.

In mid-May, Gary Carter couldn't play. He had a sore right knee; there was fluid in it and it was inflamed. He went on the disabled list, and there was the possibility that he'd be out for a long time, not just the 15 days on the list.

We made five errors against the Padres, and they beat us 4–3 at Shea. I went 0–5 and made one of the errors. It wasn't a happy day.

On May 14, I complained again about the pain in my right shoulder. We beat San Diego 2–1, but I sat out the game, until the eighth inning. I came on as a pinch hitter, with the bases loaded, one out and the score tied. I popped up to third.

We won the game, but Davey Johnson wasn't happy.

"I can't figure it out," he told the press. "This is the best offensive club I've had in my six years here, better than last year. But we're not scoring runs. And that's part of a larger scenario: not scoring runs, making mistakes on the bases, playing sloppy baseball. We're very fortunate to be where we're at."

Keith Hernandez said, "We're getting by. We're eeking out. We're going to hit eventually. But we've always had good pitching and that's what keeps us going."

The shoulder kept bothering me. When I swung, sometimes I felt it pop. The doctor told me I should feel better, but I didn't. I was 3-for-33, and Mark Carreon filled in for me in right field.

What frustrated me was that the pain prevented me from generating bat speed. I'm a power hitter, and I have to have that bat speed, to go through the zone. When you're not healthy—and for me, a left-handed hitter, the right shoulder is vital—and you don't have strength, you have a lot of problems. You pull off the ball.

To make it worse, at various times I've had back spasms, too. They're not related to the shoulder injury, but they're another bout with pain. In fact, for the first two months of the season, I had various nagging injuries. And I wasn't the only one. The whole club had been suffering.

Tim Teufel went jogging, just a relaxed jog, and he stepped on a curb and blew out his ankle. Gary Carter's knee was a disaster. And there was more to come.

On May 15, we lost to the Dodgers in New York, 3–1. It was our first meeting since the '88 playoffs. We wanted to win it. We didn't win it. The score was tied 1–1 in the ninth.

Randy Myers, who was having a super year, gave up the winning run. Some of us remembered that in '88, we beat the Dodgers 10 out of 11 before the playoffs. I did hit my eighth homer in the May 15 game, for our only run. Before that hit, I had gone 3–35. The homer wasn't much consolation.

Two nights later, Keith Hernandez collided with the Dodger shortstop, Dave Anderson, while breaking up a double play. It was typical of Hernandez to get hurt that way. He never stopped trying to win. He fractured his right kneecap and was lost to us for eight weeks.

At about that time, Lisa filed for divorce in L.A.

We were in first by a game and a half over the Cubs, but without Carter and Hernandez, we were in trouble.

You have to be ready to lose key players, of course. And Dave Magadan's a fine hitter. But he's no Hernandez. He's not as intense as Hernandez is out there. And that makes a big difference. Our team is an aggressive team, and when you fill in with players who are laid back, that has an effect.

We weren't the old Mets team that had fire in them. Some of these young guys were really laid back. They played like they were in college, not on a major league club.

And there wasn't much Davey could do about it. He had to play with what we had. He couldn't start a fire where there wasn't one. At the major league level, you should have fire in you; it's what separates the average ball players from the great ball players. Our pitchers have that fire, but the guys on the field behind them, well, some of them didn't have it.

Elster is young. Jefferies is 21. Magadan is young. They're all just getting their feet wet. So with Carter and Hernandez out, I had to be the one to provide the fire. Dykstra had some and so did Hojo. But the rest were just going through the motions.

Just another day at the old ball park. The young guys get down on themselves, too. They get down when they don't get hits. You can't allow that.

On May 19, we won one against the Giants in 10 innings at Shea. I got a bases-loaded walk from Goose Gossage to give us the win. I had homered in the sixth.

A week later, the Cubs were in first and we were 1½ games out. San Diego beat us 2–1 in San Diego. Ed Whitson went to 7–2 with a 2.27 ERA. In the eighth inning, with Mark Davis in relief of Whitson, I came up with a runner on first and two out. Davis struck me out on three pitches.

I guess I was trying to make contact, no matter what. In a panic. Trying too hard. It's so difficult when you're the one who has to do it all the time.

Gary Carter was due to come off the disabled list, but he wasn't ready. He needed surgery on his knee. That left it to me to be the club's inspiration. I try to do that all the time, of course, but I couldn't fire up guys who didn't have it in them. I'm not a cheerleader; that's not the way to inspire. I want the other guys to believe in what they can do. That's how I inspire. If I can communicate that, if that attitude is obvious in the field, it'll make the team a winner.

The Cubs were still ahead, but only by a half game as we moved toward the end of May. We were in L.A. Bobby Ojeda pitched a seven-hitter, a complete game—his first since the trouble with his finger. We beat the Dodgers, and Orel Hershiser, 8–2. I drove in three runs with two doubles, and we knocked out Hershiser after five innings.

The truth is that I've never had a lot of trouble facing Hershiser. I hit him well in the playoffs in '88. But he's a smart pitcher. His head keeps working when he's on the mound. He knows which guys he doesn't want to beat him. He knows which guys not to make mistakes on. In that game, he was trying to get ahead on the count. He didn't want to fall behind and let me sit on a good pitch I was looking for.

So I jumped on him early in the count. I didn't wait.

Toward the end of May, we weren't hitting. We lost seven out of nine games and scored just 26 runs in that stretch.

Ron Darling told a reporter, "This is a team in transition. The computer says that this team is as good a hitting team as anybody in the league. But computers don't hit."

On May 29, the Giants beat us, 3–2, in San Francisco. Ron Darling gave up two earned runs and lost the game. I had two hits, including a double, but it wasn't enough.

After the game, Darling told the press, "We're just not manufacturing any runs. I really don't care what's going on and how they feel back in New York. The fans are going to be in an uproar, but we just have to work out of it as best we can."

Joe Durso, reporting on the team for the *New York Times*, wrote after that 3–2 loss to the Giants, "The pain poured over the Mets in waves today: Gary Carter underwent surgery on his right knee and will be gone nearly two months. Davey Johnson will try to avoid or delay surgery on the two ruptured disks in his back, but does not know if he can. The hitters have collectively been so weak that the brass will hold a series of summit meetings this week to try to head off a collapse."

Greg Jefferies was hitting .185 and was making errors.

"I'm sick and tired of struggling every day," he said.

"The bottom line is the hitters are struggling," Darling said. "But if they're struggling, I'm struggling. You win as a team and lose as a team."

Word was out that something was going to be done. The Mets were going to call up some players or were going to trade some. Nobody knew for sure yet. But the idea wasn't exactly comforting to the team.

The guys who feel worst when there's talk about trades are the young ones. There's more for them to think about anyway. They've got enough problems out there just trying to perform.

If you're going to make changes, don't leak it to the press. Don't make the guys on the team worry about it before it happens. When a guy hears his name mentioned in a possible trade, he comes to the park, and he doesn't know if he's going to be with the team or not, and he's likely to say, what difference does it make how I play?

Things didn't get better.

We lost again to the Giants in San Francisco, 10–3. Sid Fernandez pitched in relief and gave up a three-run homer to Will Clark. Roger McDowell gave up another three-run homer, to Ernest Riles. We were all frustrated.

Howard Johnson spoke up.

"It's very frustrating," he told Joe Durso. "It wears on you. A team that scores a lot of runs one year and then doesn't.

"As a team, we've got the blahs. We're also not close. We like each other, but the closeness isn't the same. Maybe we're spoiled by the success of the last five years and we expect too much."

Hojo wondered if there was a shakeup coming. "Maybe they should do something drastic to shake things up," he said.

"No decisions yet," Davey announced.

But he did his analysis: "The best players we've got in our own organization are already here. And you could go down the list of every other club and find guys who would help you, but the cost would be out of sight. I don't see any trade happening in the next couple of weeks.

"I think it's unfair to place the blame on the little guys here when it's obvious the production of Darryl Strawberry and Kevin McReynolds is down. Strawberry's hitting

.200 with runners in scoring positions; Jefferies is hitting .250. Am I opposed to sending the kid back? You bet I am. I'm as confident he'll straighten out as the other guys. Case closed."

"It's killing me not to be helping this team," Jefferies said.

Hojo talked about the blahs. He was right. The guys respected each other, but the desire wasn't there. Without it, we're a mediocre club.

I couldn't say much to defend myself, either. I was hitting .239 in early June.

I told one reporter, "If Hernandez were here, he'd be the man making things happen. He's not, so I have to be the one to make things happen."

I have a lot of pride in winning. Keith is the same way. Some of the guys on the team were doubting themselves. I could see it in their faces. On the field, sometimes they didn't communicate with each other. All the negative publicity had messed with Jefferies' head. He couldn't stop thinking about it, and it was affecting his play in the field. He wasn't being aggressive. He and Elster would look at each other: who's going to cover second?

The season moved along.

My shoulder felt better; I worked on it. The

back spasms showed up once in a while, then disappeared. I tried not to think too much about the divorce. And I got in touch with my father, Henry.

It began with something I thought about— that you can't carry around hard feelings forever. That's life. You grow up, you look at the way things turn out. If it weren't for my father, I wouldn't even be in this world.

I started calling him, just to say hello. I would talk to him and see how things were going. We didn't talk about years ago. I'd rather not do that. I want to go on with my life. The past happened, that's all. He hasn't said anything about it either.

I think when he looks back, he must realize what a good family he had, the way all of his kids turned out. I guess he couldn't see it then, because we were all young when he left home.

My brothers and sisters did track him down. I was the one who really didn't want to see him for a long time. I think I was hurt more by the whole situation than the rest of them.

But I'm talking to him again, and that seems like the right thing to do.

Meanwhile, the team continued to have its troubles.

On June 5, we got butchered by the Cubs,

15–3. David Cone lasted just two innings, giving up seven runs. The game was over then. Even my old minor league buddy Lloyd McClendon drove in two runs. Greg Maddux was the winning pitcher, but he left after five innings when a ball I hit bounced off his leg. It wasn't a hit. In fact, I didn't have a hit all day.

The next day the Cubs did it again, beating us 8–4. The home fans were wild. The Cubs had 15 hits and 2 homers and went 9 games over .500 for the first time in two years. We did get a triple play, but that was a small reward in a losing cause. The Cubs played well—and were without outfielders Andre Dawson and rookie Jerome Walton. Bobby Ojeda took the loss, giving up nine hits and six earned runs in four innings. I had two hits, including my thirteenth homer. It didn't help.

We bounced back the next day, to beat the Cubs 10–5. Davey changed the lineup, shook it up. Hojo led off. Mookie Wilson played against a right-handed pitcher, Rick Sutcliffe. Mookie batted fifth, behind me. Two rookies, Gregg Jefferies and Jeff McKnight, started.

"I was fooling around with the lineup last night," Davey said. "I decided to mix things up instead of trying to be logical. I'd already used up my logic."

Kevin McReynolds and I were in our usual spots.

Sutcliffe can be tough, but his fast ball wasn't sinking the way it can. In Wrigley Field, when the wind is blowing out, balls fly; it's a small park. And Sutcliffe threw one to Kevin that he hit out for three runs.

Doc was pitching for us, and he gave up four runs in the third and left after five, still getting the win. Aguilera relieved and held the Cubs to just two hits.

Hojo hit his 12th homer. I didn't get a hit.

The next day, the Cubs came alive again and beat us 5–4. Ron Darling gave up four of the runs, but the winning run came in the tenth inning off of Don Aase. Lloyd McClendon homered. So did Hojo and McReynolds, but it wasn't enough for us to come out on top. I went hitless again.

We went from Chicago to Pittsburgh, but the mood didn't change.

Pittsburgh got a run in the 10th inning, and they beat us 4–3. We helped them end their seven-game losing streak. I hit a homer. It was my 14th of the season and the 200th of my career. I wanted to celebrate, but it was not a time for a celebration.

That day, the club traded Terry Leach to

the Kansas City Royals and recalled David West, a young left-handed pitcher, from Tidewater.

Leach was a quiet pro who went about his work with a special determination. He wasn't a kid; he'd been around for years. But he did his job.

It was a surprise when Terry was traded. He was a guy who never said much around the clubhouse, but he went out and did his job. The mood the day we got the word was a little strange. But guys were forced to say what was true, that Terry had been traded and we had to continue to go out there and do our best. Every guy went up to Terry and wished him the best of luck and we meant it. I knew we'd miss him.

We were in third place on June 9, three-and-a-half games behind the Cubs and one-and-a-half games behind Montreal. We were hanging in, despite our troubles. But there wasn't too much to be proud of.

By June 11, we were into a three-game losing streak. That ended in Pittsburgh. Bobby Ojeda pitched a six-hitter and Lenny Dykstra hit a two-run homer, to lead us to a 6–1 win. I singled in a run and Hojo homered, his fifteenth of the season and fourth in five games. Hojo was coming alive. Gregg Jefferies was turning it around, too. He had nine hits in his last sixteen at-bats.

We got back to Shea to confront the Cubs again. This time, we were prepared. It was one of those rainy games that go on and on. This one went into the 12th inning, when Jefferies hit a single to drive in the winning run. We had to use six pitchers. I hit a homer, my 15th, off lefty Steve Wilson. Final score: 4–3.

On June 19, we were two games behind the Cubs and the team made a move.

According to rumors, the Mets had tried to get Joe Carter or Danny Tartabull or Ellis Burks, but didn't. So they sent Lenny Dykstra and Roger McDowell to the Phillies for Juan Samuel. Samuel had been a second baseman who the Phillies had shifted to center field. Davey announced that Samuel would play center for us.

Lenny, who didn't like being platooned in center, would become the Phillies' regular center fielder.

Lenny told a reporter, "I'll miss the guys, but I'm not sad. It was time to make a move. It's time to show I can hit left-handed pitching. I'm looking forward to playing every day."

Roger had his say: "I'll really miss leaving the guys. I've been here four and a half years and we've had a lot of success. I'm looking forward to getting a chance to pitch."

Nick Leyva, the Phillies' manager, said that "Len Dykstra will play every day no matter who's pitching and be our leadoff hitter. McDowell will be a closer. He's a durable, steady guy."

One day, the guys are in the Mets' clubhouse; the next day, they're gone. If you're a pro, and I am, you know that's part of baseball. But you never quite get used to it.

That trade, for me, wasn't exactly like seeing Terry Leach go. Those guys, Dykstra and McDowell, had been with the team for a long time. They got recognition for being outstanding players. They were friends of all the guys on the team.

The truth is that we got an excellent player in Juan Samuel. I knew it would be just a matter of time before he got accustomed to playing in New York. Some people thought it was an unfair trade, that we got less than we gave. But we didn't. Dykstra wanted to play every day, and it was a good opportunity for him to do that. McDowell was having some rough times with us. It was good for them to get away and start a new life and go on with their careers.

I talked to both of them before they left. They weren't bitter. It was a sad moment, but they understood that baseball is a business and that the trade could be a turnaround for them. It's important to think about that; you have to think about your career, where it's going. Trades happen every day. But you hate to be traded after you've developed a relationship with a ball club.

We were still in third place, behind the Cubs and Montreal, as June moved along. We were hanging in, but we didn't seem able to get that burst that would carry us past the other teams in contention.

Montreal came into Shea. We led 5–0 after one inning. That was the end of our run production for the night. We lost the game 8–5.

The night before that, Montreal pitcher Kevin Gross had thrown a ball at my feet. It hit my small right toe and fractured it. More pain, more frustration, more time out of the lineup.

I was hitting .224, with 15 homers and 33 RBIs.

The last place I wanted to be was on the disabled list. So I walked around as well as I could and waited for the pain to stop and the healing to begin. When I could put my shoe back on, I knew I was making progress.

I didn't play, but we beat the Phillies again on June 23. Bobby Ojeda beat them again, for the second time in a week. Hojo had two

RBIs. He had 9 homers and 18 RBIs in his last 20 games.

Lenny Dykstra hit a triple to drive in a run. He was 7 for 16 with 7 runs scored since joining the Phillies. We won the game, so I could be happy for him.

We swept a three-game series at Shea against the Phillies with a 5–1 win. Sid Fernandez got the win. Gregg Jefferies had three hits, a single, a double and a triple, in four at-bats, and drove in two runs. It was an unusual game for one reason: we tied a 44-year-old record by getting all 27 outs without an assist. Fernandez struck out nine and Aguilera added four. The Phillies had 12 fly ball outs and two grounders to first. Not a single assist. It was the first in National League history and the first in the majors since 1945, when Cleveland did it against the Yankees.

I was still waiting to play, but the team was winning again. And we were tied with the Cubs for the division lead.

On June 26, we were in Montreal to take on the Expos. If the Cubs faded—and they had faded in mid-summer in the past—and the Cardinals didn't have enough for the long season, the Expos would be the team we would have to beat to win the title.

But on that night, Doc lasted only four innings; he'd been bothered by shoulder stiffness in his two previous starts. He allowed a three-run homer to Spike Owens, not a player known to hit homers. And Montreal won it, 5–1. Pascual Perez, a smart veteran pitcher, allowed us just five hits and struck out eleven. Gregg Jefferies had to leave the game when he got dizzy after running into Andres Galarraga at first base. And catcher Barry Lyons had to leave when he was hit by a foul ball on his right big toe.

They'd both get better quickly. Maybe the injury problems would ease up. That's what I thought. I was feeling better. And given enough time to heal, Carter and Hernandez would be back. If we were lucky, they'd be back before the season ended.

The Expos didn't seem to care, however. They beat us again, 3–2, the next night. They passed us and the Cubs and went into first place. The game went 14 innings. Both teams had chances to win it. The Expos cashed in, when Tim Wallach singled home Nelson Santovenia in the 14th. Mookie Wilson filled in for me in right, and I got to pinch-hit, but without success.

The next night, the Expos rubbed it in. We got our first look at left-hander Mark Langston, the pitcher the Expos got from Seattle. We got 12 hits off him in 8 innings, but he struck out 10 Mets and was on top when it was over, the Expos winning 4–3. It was a sweep of the three-game series for the Expos. They moved two-and-a-half games in front of us and the Cubs. Bobby Ojeda lost again. Mookie, in right field for me, went 1–5. I didn't get into the game. My toe continued to ache, but I could feel that it was getting better.

I was eager to get back into the lineup, as the teams all moved toward the All-Star break. It was too early to be discouraged, either about my injuries or about the way the team had played during the first half of the season. There was time to heal and plenty of time left to win.

I still believed that we could beat Montreal, which seemed like the team to beat at that point in the season. The Cubs were up there, and St. Louis couldn't be counted out, either. In mid-season, I still felt that we could beat anybody. Our club, I believed, was a very competent ball club. If you looked at what the club had done over the last five years, we always had a winning record.

We won it all in '86. We lost in '87, but we also lost our whole pitching staff that year. Everybody got hurt. Then, we came back in '88 and won our division, only to lose to the Dodgers. Every year, the Mets are the team that's favored to win. We have the talent to put on the field every day. We produce. We are known for winning.

I felt that this year we were going through something for the first time: There were different players, younger players. They weren't like veterans, who know what it's like to be out there under pressure and to win. You have to be intense at this level. This season, we had some kids who hadn't been through the fire. They were kids with great talent, but this was their first real test, and they were learning what it's like to go through rough times.

Sometimes, it got me down when we didn't play as well as I thought we could. I told a reporter, "We don't want to win. Half the time, the guys don't care. They're just going through the motions. These guys just want to sit around and play cards. I went out and played with a broken toe. We've got guys who don't take care of themselves. Our pitching's not the problem. The guys have to prove to themselves that they're capable of winning. It's a shame the way our offense has been."

I was really talking about pride. You have to take pride in what you do, whatever you're doing. If you take pride in your work and you're very dedicated, you're going to do it well.

We were in the middle of a pennant race, and there was no question about it, we couldn't sit back and wait for it to happen. We had to make it happen. I wasn't knocking any particular player; we were all in it together.

I'm the kind of player who's always loved to win, to go out there and compete at my best. There was a difference, though, between the '89 Mets and the Mets of the previous few years. I've won with this ball club, and I know what kind of attitude it takes to win. During the season in '89, I watched that winning chemistry change. The killer instinct wasn't there, and that was contagious; I lost a little bit myself. Even my attention level went down. I always believed we could come from behind to win, but some of the young guys didn't understand that yet.

After being out for about 10 days with my broken toe, I got back into the lineup at the end of June in Cincinnati. It was a game we won 11–1 in an unusual way, with three three-run homers, by me, Hojo and, of all people, Ron Darling. My first time up I struck out, though.

After you spend time on the bench and you get back up there for the first time, you're a little overanxious. I didn't feel relaxed. Ten ball games are a lot to miss.

Then, we were into July. The season was moving along, although there were plenty of games left.

Doc Gooden had to come out in the third inning of our 6–2 loss to Cincinnati. He had "soreness in his right armpit" and couldn't get loose, before the game or during the game. When he was asked how he felt, Doc said, "You don't feel a sharp pain from throwing. It's as if someone hit you with a stick or a hammer." Doc had to go on the DL.

I wasn't aware of just how serious his injury was. The only player who's ever aware of how bad an injury hurts is the one who feels the pain. But when I'm out there in right field, watching the pitcher throw, I can tell if he's having problems. He might be favoring something, not really cutting it loose.

I got a double in that game in which Doc was hurt, but it didn't help. We still lost.

One day my toe would feel fine; the next day it would hurt again. Mark Carreon subbed for me in Houston, and he hit a homer. David Cone got to 5–5 with a 3–1 win over the Astros. I had to stay out of the lineup, except to pinch-hit, until after the All-Star break. Davey Johnson and I talked about it, and that seemed like the best thing to do.

On July 4th, I was hitting .224. Not good. But I didn't want to let it get me down. It was the first time that I'd really ever struggled like that. It boiled down to the injuries. They make a big difference in your performance. You know that you can't do the things you really want to do. I wanted to go to bat and be aggressive, but I couldn't. I was playing with a broken toe. I really couldn't drive off my lead foot the way I needed to. I struggled. The series of injuries was the most I'd ever had in a season. I had missed about 25 games by July. And I wasn't ever on the DL.

On July 5th, the doctors diagnosed Doc's injury as a small muscle tear, and they said he'd be off for three to four weeks and had to rest. That was like a kick to the rest of us.

You know that injuries are a part of the game, of course. If you're all healthy, the ball club does well. If you lose key players, things can go bad.

Everytime you're injured, you've got a new problem to solve. When I injured my shoulder swinging at that Ontiveros pitch, I had to take it slow. It was one of those nagging problems. It wasn't a serious injury, but it was one of those injuries that could hamper the kind of swing I take, driving the ball. I just had to take it slowly and let the injury go away by itself. There's nothing you can do for an injury like that. Just rest it. No swinging, no hitting, nothing.

Then, I had back spasms. You don't do much for those, either. Rest. Ice. Ultrasound. Mostly, though, it takes time.

When I broke my little toe, that was the injury that really put a hurting on me. I couldn't move on that toe without real pain. I couldn't run at all. Part of my game was taken away from me—no stealing bases. That, too, was one of those injuries requiring rest. I tried to come back and play with the painful toe, but then I had to sit down again. If you come back too soon, you can hurt another part of your body just trying to compensate for the toe. You can put pressure on your other leg.

Meanwhile, the All-Star balloting was going on and I finished second to Kevin Mitchell in the voting. I guess the fans realized that I'd put out some big numbers year after year, even if my stats in '89 weren't so great. I guess they said, he's hit more than 20 home runs every year in his major league career.

During the season, when you're in the pennant race, you think about each game and what you've got to do. But you still pay attention to what's going on in the rest of the league. Last season, I watched Kevin Mitchell become a major league star. I knew him, from the minors and the Mets, and I was very glad to see him reach his potential. It happens with some players. You get to that stage in your career where you're very relaxed about yourself, very confident about your ability to play the game. I think that's what really happened to Kevin.

Kevin's had some tough times in his personal life. Gangs, when he was growing up on the west coast, and in New York he couldn't seem to get himself on the right track off the field. Too many temptations. The New York lifestyle can destroy a player. Then he went back to his home town, San Diego, which was a mess for him because that's where he grew up and he was surrounded by all the same things that had once gotten him in trouble. Guys with bad intentions come out of hiding when you show up like that.

So it was good for him to get to San Francisco. There he could relax, play baseball, just concentrate on living a healthy life.

Of course, players don't get a reputation for being a star just by one year. You have to pile the years together and look at the numbers.

On July 7th, Sid Fernandez went to 7–2 and pitched a three-hitter and beat the Reds

7–1 at Shea. It broke a three-game losing streak for us. Bobby Ojeda, Ron Darling and Dave West had allowed 20 earned runs in just over 9 innings. Somebody asked Fernandez after the game what he had done to win. He said, "I just throw the ball." I got a double and split right field with Mookie Wilson.

It was almost time to rest, for the All-Star break.

I would have loved to play in that game again, because the fans selected me. But I had to be realistic about it. It was Davey Johnson's decision, actually, but we had talked about it. He said he didn't want me to play in the All-Star game because we had the second half of the season ahead of us and it was important for me to rest. If I went to the game, there'd be so much excitement there that I might get out on the field and try to do something I shouldn't do and reinjure myself. So I stayed at home in New York. It boils down to this: your team comes first. I had to respect my importance to the team. I didn't play in the game, but I got to relax, and that turned out to be good for me and for the team.

Just before the break, I got back into the lineup and I went wild. I got three hits, including a two-run homer, my 17th in a win over the Reds. David Cone went to 6–5. There was a brawl when Rob Dibble hit Tim Teufel. After the game, Pete Rose said that we had a big lead but were stealing bases. When that happens, he said, "you should expect to get knocked down."

Fair enough, maybe. But if we did steal a base, why didn't Dibble drill the guy who stole the base instead of the guy who had nothing to do with it?

Anyway, Juan Samuel came out and got into the fight, and some of the Reds remembered that. After the game, Reds' pitcher Norm Charlton called the Mets clubhouse looking for Samuel. I was the one who answered the phone. I told Charlton to come on over.

There he was, a rookie pitcher, with the nerve to call our clubhouse, to call a bunch of winners who knew what it was all about. A fight is a fight, and you leave it on the field. You don't call the clubhouse looking for anyone.

Charlton and Danny Jackson and Tom Browning apparently were all heading over to our clubhouse looking for trouble. We were heading under the stands to meet them. Security guys headed them off.

The whole incident was a rookie mistake. Rookie pitchers, sometimes, are on an ego trip. They get up to this level and they feel they're the stuff. They have to realize that you don't mess with a bunch of veteran players who've been around. You never bring a fight into the opposing team's clubhouse. When you do that, you better be ready to fight the whole ball club.

The next day, we did it our way. We beat the Reds—Dibble, Charlton and the rest—at Shea, 6–3. Samuel got a hit off of Dibble. "That evened things," Juan said. I had a double and drove in a run. There wasn't any more trouble, by the way, and that had to do with an order from the league president, who told both teams that if there was any more violence, there'd be a lot of suspensions.

We got the word that Keith Hernandez, in rehab with our team in Port St. Lucie, Florida, went 3-for-4 in a Class A game. We were just two-and-a-half games behind Montreal, and the idea of having Mex back felt good.

On July 9th, the news was about Hojo. The Mets signed him to a three-year, $6,100,000 contract. He was hitting .293, with 22 homers, 57 RBIs and 18 stolen bases at the time. He'd come a long way from almost being traded in spring training.

I didn't make any comparisons with my own contract; Hojo's good news didn't annoy me at all. He was going to become a free agent at the end of the year if they didn't sign him.

They talked about trading him in the spring, because he had had a bad year and had a bad shoulder. All of a sudden, he comes back, is healthy and has an outstanding first half. Hojo could have waited and negotiated after he became a free agent, but he decided not to. I didn't talk to him about it. I just congratulated him.

After the All-Star game, we put together a four-game winning streak. We beat the Braves 5–1, with Ron Darling pitching a five-hitter and going 7–6. Hernandez was back and got an RBI single. "It's like opening day," he said. "I felt a little sluggish. The last at-bat I was tired. I have to build up my stamina." I hit my 18th homer off of Pete Smith.

It was good to see Mex back. Just the presence of him in the lineup made the lineup stronger. He can perform.

The next day, Sid Fernandez struck out 16 Braves, the most strikeouts he'd ever had, and lost the game to the Braves 3–2 when Lonnie Smith hit a homer in the ninth.

Sid pitched a game in which he'd done everything right. He just went right after the hitters. It was an exciting performance, but we just couldn't put our offense together to produce any runs. And Lonnie Smith had struck out three times before he hit the homer. He's got nine lives.

On July 15th, we beat the Braves again, 6–4. I hit my 19th homer.

Then, things went a little sour. We lost two to the Astros in a doubleheader at Shea. It was the first doubleheader we had lost at Shea in almost four years. I went 0-for-3 in the first game and sat out the second game. We were five games behind the Expos.

I was still having trouble with my toe. And batting against Jim Deshaies didn't help. He's a sneaky type pitcher. His ball gets up on you before you know it. He's not overpowering, but he gets a lot of strikeouts because his delivery is strange and it's hard to pick up the ball.

After that doubleheader, Davey Johnson told the press, "Things have been very rough and I'm extremely concerned. We're losing with our pitching. That was supposed to be our strength and there's nothing much I can do about it."

I had to agree with him. If our pitching went bad, we would be in serious trouble. We didn't have anyone down at Tidewater we could bring up. We had to get our pitchers on the right track, and we did, when Sid Fernandez shut out the Astros 9–0. Unfortunately, Mex bruised his bad knee and had to leave the game.

Davey had a talk with the team, and he was just trying to get the guys to know that we had to be more intense on the field. Davey didn't criticize individuals. But if you're one of the main guys on the team, a guy who's got a more-than-a-million dollar contract, you knew who he was talking to. When you win for years and get paid for winning, you know when you aren't delivering as expected.

Davey explained it to us as a matter of confidence and concentration. That was his message.

We went out and beat the Astros again, 8–2, with David Cone pitching a complete game. I had my 20th homer and a pair of RBIs.

July was moving along. On the 20th, we beat the Braves 4–1, Bobby Ojeda's first win in five starts since late June. I got my 21st homer, a double, and batted in three runs. There were a couple of rain delays in that game; I hit the homer after one long one.

Rain delays can drive you up a wall, because you are forced to wait and to think. You sit in the clubhouse and you try to relax. You just wait for the umpires to let you know it's time to start again. When they do, you're supposed to crank it up. It's strange.

The next day, we beat the Braves again, 6–4, and I got my 22nd homer, a single and two RBIs. I had 18 RBIs in my last 16 games. I didn't have much pain left in my toe. I certainly didn't feel it when I was batting.

I still wasn't hitting for average, batting .236 in late July. We lost to the Pirates and Doug Drabek at Shea, 4–2. Ojeda gave up just three hits and one earned run in seven innings. I had a double and an RBI, but they weren't enough. Drabek is the kind of pitcher who picks his spots. That's his secret. When you have good control, the way he does, you don't have to be overpowering. You can finesse pitch.

That day something else happened. The team put Lee Mazzilli on wavers and activated Gary Carter.

Frank Cashen told the press, "We felt we had to keep Mark Carreon. We felt we had a better chance of winning with him." Lee said, "When I came into this organization, I was a baby, 17, 18-years-old. It's like a relationship with a brother or sister."

I didn't have a special relationship with Lee. We were just teammates. He went about his business. He had a long relationship with the Mets, of course, and while you hate to see that come to an end, it's part of the business, and you really don't have any control over it.

We lost Lee, but we regained Gary. That seemed to me to be progress.

But it didn't translate into wins on the field. The Pirates beat us again at Shea, 10–8. They swept a three-game series in New York for the first time in eight years. It was a hot day, 92 degrees, and there was a 45-minute rain delay, a chance to appreciate the humidity. We used six pitchers.

That kind of day drains you. The air is heavy. It's hard on you, running out there, swinging the bat. Your body starts to slow down.

That was the day, too, that the rumors started about the Mets getting Frank Viola. When I first heard it, I really didn't think too much about it. Trade rumors come and go. I was telling myself, we've got outstanding pitchers. It doesn't matter who they bring in if the chemistry isn't there. You win as a unit. I knew that Frank Viola was an outstanding pitcher and that he could help us. But I wondered if one player could make the difference in how the club performed.

At the same time, Gary Carter was back in the lineup. He couldn't get a hit, and the fans at Shea were booing him. That bothered me. Sure, you get booed at home. But we were guys who had achieved so much for those fans over the past five years. Guys were reaching low points in their careers. I was probably at my lowest point. I was having a terrible year, but I knew that I'd improve. When Gary got booed, I thought that the fans should learn to appreciate what he had contributed in his years on the Mets and accept it. He wasn't up to par, but he was still out there trying for the organization.

As for the team, we were moving toward August, when the race gets hot. I knew I was a much better hitter than I had been up to that point in the season. You go through those spells, where the pressure is all on you. Nobody knows that feeling unless they've gone through it.

I've hit well when I've had guys surrounding me, like Hernandez, Carter. It's always made me more relaxed. We were going through a summer when we didn't have those hitters to provide the protection, make more opportunities for me to relax and do my job. I was trying to do too much.

As July came to an end, we were five games out behind the Expos and the Cubs with a three-game series coming up against the Cubs in Chicago. We didn't take the Cubs lightly. You have to give the organization credit for getting some young players who can play. The Cubs made the decision to bring up the young guys, to play them at the major league level and live with them, suffer with them, die with them if that's how it had to be. In my opinion, when those young players have talent and you let them learn to play in the majors and grow into who they can be, they eventually become winners.

At that point, I thought the race would be a real dogfight. I didn't think that we were out of it. I knew the kind of ball club that we had, a unique ball club. I believed that we had more talent than any club in the east.

Meanwhile, on the newsstands, the latest issue of *Playboy* had an interview with Hernandez in which he talked about me. He talked about his special attachment to me, and about the "intense, immense pressure" put on me from the day I came to the Mets. He said a lot of kind things.

Keith and I always had a great relationship. We were two leaders on the team, the backbone that kept the club together, made it want to win. The media hype in New York has tried to destroy relationships between certain players. Well, Keith plays to win and so do I. That's been his attitude all the years I've known him. When I had super years, I was having them because I was learning from him. Our friendship survived all the hype and bad stuff written about us. Headlines make ball players who have great personalities look like assholes.

When you play together as Mex and I did, you're both out there to do the same thing: win. Winning is contagious, and we were used to winning. Our whole club stayed together. Over the years, we were the team that was close, known to pick each other up. When a guy was going bad, you'd take him out to dinner, have a few drinks, give him a good time. We always believed that better times were ahead.

I still believe that.

In Chicago, at the end of July, it didn't work out that way.

We lost the opener to the Cubs, 6–5, a game we shouldn't have lost. The Cubs got four in the seventh to win it. We lost the next two as well, and all of a sudden we had a six-game losing streak. The Cubs were moving up, winning 10 out of 13. It was the last day of July.

Help was coming.

On the last day of July, the rumor came true. We got Frank Viola from the Twins. We gave up some pitchers, including Rick Aguilera and David West, but we got the previous season's American League Cy Young winner. Viola was born in New York, so he would feel at home with us.

Nevertheless, we lost our seventh straight game in St. Louis the next day, 3–2. It was our longest losing streak in five years.

Jose DeLeon had found out how to pitch against us—and everybody else—in 1989. In the years before that, he couldn't find a way to beat the Mets. Then he got more confidence in his pitches. He used to make a lot of mistakes, in big situations. He'd get his fork ball where he didn't want to get it. He'd give up a hit, then another, then a homer, and he'd be out of the game. He had a head game going. It was a challenge he had to face, to concentrate. He did that and now he's a winner.

We broke out of the losing streak, in style, the next day, when we beat the Cards 11–0. Kevin McReynolds hit for the cycle and drove in six runs (his career high). Sid Fernandez pitched a four-hitter. But all the news wasn't good. We sent Mookie Wilson to the Toronto Blue Jays for pitcher Jeff Musselman. Mookie had been with the Mets for 10 years; he had more service with the team than anyone on the current roster. He was a class act and I knew I would miss him.

I'm sure that some players worry about being traded, but I never have. I've had times, in my own mind, when I've considered that I would like to be traded. But being traded by the Mets, without expecting it, well, I think I could handle that.

My reaction would be, well, I've enjoyed my career in New York. I don't have any regrets about the New York fans. I've always respected them. I think the only reason that negative things have happened is because of the New York media hype. That destroys relationships between fans and players, which is not good.

But if I got the word that I'd been traded, I'd say that life goes on and I have to go on from there. It wouldn't matter to me what team I was traded to. I would go with the same attitude, starting new and performing, making the best out of it.

The next night Viola pitched against the Cards and we got three runs in the ninth to get him his first win for us, 4–3. Samuel batted in one of those runs, and Kevin McReynolds knocked in the other two to win it.

But we were still in fourth place, 6½ games behind Montreal. The next day we went to seven games behind when the Cards beat us 6–5. I got a hit and scored a run. That doesn't mean much when you lose, but we were on our way back to Shea to play the Expos.

A few hours before that first night game, general manager Frank Cashen had a team meeting. He told us that Doc wouldn't be back soon, but that we had the talent to win the pennant—and it was time for us to start showing it.

Cashen's meeting seemed like a way of telling us that the club believed in the players and it would do whatever it could to help us win. He said they'd trade for guys, release guys, whatever it took. We were playing hard, of course, and maybe the front office didn't realize that as good as a club might be, there are times when things just don't work out as they should. It's not as if the players weren't going out there giving their best. When guys are having off seasons, and I surely was, it's not that they aren't trying. They are, but the trying doesn't seem to make a difference. Anyway, after that talk, we had to show something on the field.

We did. We beat Montreal 11–5. Hojo had a three-run homer and Juan Samuel had three hits. I had three hits, too. Bobby Ojeda got the win. We chopped a game off of Montreal's lead and we were beginning to feel good again.

The next day, we beat them again, 3–2. Ron Darling pitched a six-hitter. We were behind 2–1 while Mark Langston was in the game, but when he left after seven innings, we jumped on Tim Burke for two runs and

204

the win. Montreal manager Buck Rodgers told a sportswriter, "We used to figure the key to beating the Mets was to keep Lenny Dykstra, Wally Backman and Mookie Wilson off base. Now they're all gone." Maybe Rodgers noticed that the guys who were left could play, too.

It took 14 innings the next day for us to sweep the Expos, 2–1. Kevin McReynolds led off the 14th with a homer to do it. Kevin Gross had a 1–0 lead in the seventh when I hit one out to tie it. It was my 23rd homer. I had four RBIs and six runs scored in my last five games. We were four games out of first and moving.

In his second start for us, Frank Viola went against the Phillies in Philadelphia and lost 2–1, although he allowed just five hits and struck out eight and walked one in seven innings. We just couldn't do much against Ken Howell. That was the end of our three-game winning streak.

I felt the pressure. You always do. I told the press that I wouldn't be talking to them for the rest of the season because I felt that I'd been unfairly blamed for all of the Mets' problems. When I said it, I believed it. That's how I felt. I was tired of getting all the blame. Every little thing that happened, every game we lost, the writers were writing that I didn't come through, didn't get the big hit. I wasn't the only guy on the club who was not playing up to his potential. It takes more than one player to make a ball club go. The writers would say that when I hit, the Mets won. It wasn't always going to be like that. I told them to look back at the years I had when the Mets still didn't win. Only when the whole team works together do you win. Of course, I wasn't ready to write off the season.

I felt that my game was gaining some energy, but I was still hitting .234 and that didn't make me very happy.

We came back the next day against the Phillies. David Cone shut them out, I hit a three-run homer, my 24th, and we won it, 9–0. The Cubs helped by beating Montreal 4–2. We were five out of first.

Somebody showed me a story in the paper that read, "The pitching is back and so is Darryl Strawberry." Gary Carter was back, too, with 4-for-4 as we beat the Phillies again behind Bobby Ojeda's shutout, 6–0. I had a two-run homer. I was 11-for-31 in August, with three homers, two doubles and nine RBIs. Unlike past seasons, when I got a little tired in August, I was determined to keep my energy level up during that hot month.

We went back home for a doubleheader with the Cards. In the first game, Ron Darling won 5–1. In the second, we won 6–4. We went to three-and-a-half games behind the Cubs. "This is just what we needed to get us back into it," Davey Johnson said. "The feeling I get is that we are having fun."

But the next day, we stumbled. The Cards beat us, and Viola, 3–0. Scott Terry and Ken Dayley allowed us just three hits.

The night after that, we got back on track. David Cone won his seventh straight, 3–1, over the Cards at Shea. David got three hits. Whitey Herzog said afterward, "Too much David Cone pitching and hitting."

That Sunday we made it four-out-of-five against the Cards when Bobby Ojeda beat them 3–2. We had won 11 out of 14 and had closed to within three games in the loss column against the Cubs. I had a triple in that one.

San Diego came to Shea, and we opened the series with a 3–2 win. Kevin McReynolds tied the game in the ninth with a homer, and Kevin Elster won it with an RBI double. We beat one of the best pitchers around, Ed Whitson. The Cubs won, too, and stayed three-and-a-half ahead of us, but the Expos fell into third, losing their 10th in 12 games. The race was a tight one, and it looked as if the winning team would be the one that made the fewest mistakes and played at its best all the way through the rest of the season. It wasn't a time to quit.

We stayed alive by beating the Padres 7–2. I hit two homers, the 20th time I'd done that in a game. Ron Darling was smart on the mound, as usual, and won his 11th game. It was our eighth victory in nine games. We were on a roll. Hojo hit his 29th homer, and I had 27. "I've said all along, Darryl Strawberry is the most feared hitter in the lineup," Davey told the press after the game. "It affects us and the way we do things, makes us more aggressive." I was happy to hear that. We were getting what we hadn't had before, an aggressive approach to the game. And we won that one despite a 93-minute rain delay.

San Diego came back and won the final game in the series, 6–2. They beat Viola, but we were still 13–4 in August.

The Dodgers came to Shea, with Orel Hershiser. We were ready and won the opener 3–2. David Cone won his eighth straight. He had to be good, because beating Hershiser isn't easy for any team. I managed to get a double off of him, and that's satisfying. "On Straw's hit, the pitch was up," Hershiser said after the game. I guess I was ready for it. What wasn't such good news was the fact that Keith Hernandez aggravated his bruised right thigh again and had to leave the game.

The next day Bobby Ojeda got back to work, winning his fifth straight by beating the Dodgers 4–1. Dave Magadan filled in for Mex and went 3-for-3 with a two-run double. Magadan doesn't like to sit on the bench— · nobody does—but he is ready when he has to play. "I try not to worry about it," he said.

That Sunday at Shea, Willie Randolph beat us with his first home run in almost a year; the Dodgers won it 5–4. We stayed two-and-a-half games behind the Cubs. We were 15–5 in August and 8–3 on the homestand with three games left at Shea.

The San Francisco Giants came to town. Ron Darling struck out ten of them, and we beat them 4–1. Greg Jefferies had three hits; he was coming out of that terrible stretch earlier in the season. Doc began to throw again in the bullpen, but the injury wasn't healed yet.

The Giants aren't a team to drop dead. The next night Kevin Mitchell hit his 40th homer, Bob Knepper allowed us just four hits, and they beat Viola and the rest of us, 5–0. At the same time, the Reds beat the Cubs, and we stayed at a game and a half out of first, with Montreal two out and the Cards just three out. It looked like the rest of the season would be a fight involving all four teams. I was still confident that we would win it all.

We went to the coast for nine games, three with San Diego, three with the Dodgers, three with the Giants. It was a crucial trip.

We lost to the Padres three straight times. It hurt. During the third game, I caught a fly ball and turned around and threw it out of the stadium. I was frustrated. I wasn't playing well, and we weren't playing well as a team.

Then, we swept three from the Dodgers and felt better. The Giants took care of that, by taking three from us. So we were 3–6 on the trip, very bad.

But we were still close to the Cubs. It wasn't over yet. Somebody had sent me a piece of crystal that was supposed to bring me good luck. I kept it with me, until I misplaced it. Frank Viola found it, in the locker room, but it must have been defective. Nothing worked for me that season.

When we lost in San Francisco, Davey Johnson called me in, just before we were heading back home to Shea. He told me that he thought that the ball club responded to the way I performed. He told me not to worry, that he understood about my personal problems. But he said I had to clear my mind of all that and go out on the field and play ball as well as I could.

But it wasn't as if I wasn't trying. My mind was clogged up with so many different things, trying to concentrate, struggling, fighting to get out of my slump. But the conversation with Davey never got unfriendly. He just wanted me to try harder, to be a little more aggressive, to take charge more than I had been. He told me that he'd never seen me as down as I was then. And he'd known me since Tidewater.

Even then, I thought the Mets could catch on fire and win it all. You always have to believe that. If you doubt yourself in the middle of a pennant race, you might as well pack your bags and go home.

As the season moved along, the Pirates gave us trouble. People wonder about that, about how a team that's out of it plays like champions at the end of the season. It happens every year. They're motivated to do well against the good teams. The intensity level rises.

To complicate it all, I still had trouble with my back, spasms that kept coming and going during the last month and a half of the season.

Davey called a team meeting, after I got back into the lineup and we opened a road trip by beating the Phillies 5–2 and going into third place, four and a half games out. He told us not to hang our heads, that it wasn't the end of the world. We're just not getting the job done, he said. It can be frustrating, not living up to expectations.

That's exactly what was happening. We really hadn't gotten the job done together. Individuals did their jobs, like Hojo, but as far as the team was concerned, no. You win a pennant when everybody does well all the time. That's why I keep saying that people didn't understand that one particular player isn't enough. They expect so much out of one particular player, but if he's not doing it, other guys have to pick it up. If that happens, the team can still win.

We were without Hernandez. Another 90 RBIs missing. A guy like Carter, even when he has an off season, he drives in 70 runs. When you don't have them on the team every day, you miss a lot of things that could win games. The guys who fill in for those experienced players are just learning what it's like to be in the middle of a pennant race. The pressure is tough for them.

Sure, we were a few games out of first as the season was moving toward the last few weeks. But figure where we would have been if Carter and Hernandez and Gooden had all been healthy and hadn't missed any games. We could have been 15 games in front.

The truth was that we did lose them and we weren't in front. In mid-September, we were five-and-a-half out of first, behind the Cubs. The Cards were hanging in, but the Expos seemed to be fading right out of it. We went to Montreal and David Cone shut them out, 5–0.

The next day, the Cubs lost and so did we, to the Expos. It was one of those chances we had to gain ground, but we didn't. As usual, the press didn't do us any favors, either.

It came out that Hojo and I criticized our teammates. What we really said was that the guys on the club were sick and tired of the New York press singling guys out and putting them down. We said that some guys wanted to go elsewhere to play, and I said I didn't blame them. I never mentioned names. Hojo said, "It takes everybody to win and we're definitely not together." I said what I had already said a couple of months before that, that a lot of guys were unhappy with what you have to deal with in New York.

Things didn't get better.

Mark Langston beat us 1–0 in Montreal.

St. Louis climbed over us into second place. We were five-and-a-half back, but time was running out, with just 14 games left. And we were going into Chicago to take on the Cubs.

Looking back at our losses in Montreal— we lost one game 10–1—Hernandez said, "It was a lost weekend. We had a chance to go into Chicago and put pressure on them. Now we've put ourselves at a great disadvantage."

Tim Teufel said, "If we keep playing the way we are, there's no hope we can even come close. I think we've proved you can't turn it off and then turn it on."

The Cubs beat us 10–6 in the first of our two games. I was depressed. I didn't think I'd bat in the ninth, so I went into the clubhouse for a break, to try to get my head together. Mitch Williams was pitching for the Cubs, and we got three hits and a walk and two runs, making me the tying run. Davey found me in the clubhouse, and we had some hard words about where I was. I came out, went up to the plate, feeling frustrated about everything that had happened that season, on and off the field. Williams was wild, but he got me on three pitches.

I can't exactly say that I was angry about everything and so I swung at those bad pitches. I guess I was out of control, not thinking about what I had to do. I was sorry about that later. I was sorry, too, about making Davey mad.

The next day we beat the Cubs 5–2. Bobby Ojeda pitched well and won his 13th game. Doc Gooden pitched four good innings in relief. Davey kept me out of the game. Punishment, I guess.

It was September 20, and we were still five-and-a-half games out.

That day, a Chicago paper reported that Kevin McReynolds and I were benched and fined by Davey for going into the clubhouse during that loss to the Cubs. "I was angry and disappointed. I've never been so upset in my life," Davey said.

We went on to St. Louis. We lost 5–3. I was back in the lineup, but I went 0–5. Then, in the next game, Sid Fernandez beat the Cards 6–1. "It was too much El Cid tonight," Whitey Herzog said after the game. I had a hit and two RBIs, but somehow, it seemed to be slipping away from us, even when we won. The Cubs were staying tough.

Back at Shea, we beat the Expos 3–2. The turnout was not heavy. Maybe the fans knew that the season was over for us. "I thought a lot of these series would be more important,"

Davey told the press, "but it wasn't meant to be."

We beat the Expos again the next day and eliminated them from the pennant race. Gary Carter had three hits and drove in five runs. He wanted to prove that he could still play, even at his age and after his injuries. He wanted to stay with the Mets, he said. I didn't know if the Mets wanted him to stay.

Davey kept me out of that 13–6 win. Mark Langston pitched against us; he left in the fourth inning.

The next day, the Expos beat us 6–5 and we were six-and-a-half behind the Cubs with seven games left to play. I hit a three-run homer, my 29th, but it was only my second since the middle of August. I knew it was the worst season I'd ever had. That day at Shea when we lost to the Expos was Fan Appreciation Day; we lost a four-run lead, and the game, and were practically out of the race.

The chase did end for us at home, when the Phillies came in and beat us 2–1. "When it's not meant to be, it's not meant to be," Bobby Ojeda said. "We had our chances," Davey told the reporters, "but we never could get something going."

We had some good games and some bad ones after that, but they didn't matter much, except for our pride. The Cubs had won it. We hadn't.

We lost to the Phillies at Shea, and Gregg Jefferies and Roger McDowell got into a fight. Two guys who had played together. That's the kind of year it had been. There was a rumor that Hernandez and Carter, who would become free agents, wouldn't be back with the Mets. The crowd at Shea cheered both of them. That's how it should have been.

There was another rumor: that Davey would go, too. He had a meeting with Frank Cashen and after it ended, Davey said, "It was an amicable meeting, but I guess they give you a big meal before they pull the trigger."

The last week of the season, all the frustration I felt came out. I was interviewed, and I said, "I want to play on the west coast. A change of scenery would be good for me. I'd really enjoy it. I'd finally relax, and play the way I'm capable of playing. I won't sign a long-term contract here, no matter what the money is. I don't want to stay here. It really bothers me the way the fans turn on you, the way the media always has its knives out for you. I'm tired of being blamed for everything that goes wrong."

I knew I had my option year left on my

Mets contract, and I was confident that if the Mets picked up my option, I'd be back with the club next season and give it my best. I'd play my heart out.

During the last days of the season, the *Village Voice* printed an article by Allen Barra about me. In it, he wrote, "Darryl Strawberry is a better ball player than Reggie (Jackson) was. He's the best player the Mets have ever had—the best ball player New York has had since Mickey Mantle peaked nearly 30 years ago. The Mets have been baseball's winningest team since he became a regular. But, like the Mets, he seems to have jumped from a confident future to a disappointing past without ever basking in the present. He's not having fun, and neither are we."

That's for sure.

It was a terrible season for me. Even a letter of encouragement from former President Nixon didn't help me. He's a fan of mine, and he's sent me letters for a couple of years. He tells me not to worry about the media, because those people are going to write what they want to write. He ought to know, I guess. He wants me to know that he thinks I'm a great ball player and not to let the fans or the press get to me. He wishes me luck, tells me he's 100 percent behind me. Cheer-up letters, that's what he sends me.

But for the '89 season, there wasn't any cheering up. We struggled as a team. We didn't play the way we should have. The chemistry wasn't there. The Cubs had the chemistry. Experienced guys and young guys working together and being happy together. We did that in the past, but not this year. And when you don't have it, you can't be successful.

Of course, we had all those injuries, including my own. And we traded some good minor league guys away. Also, the division was more balanced in '89 than it had been in years. For most of the season, the Cubs, the Cards, the Expos, the Mets were all in contention. I thought we had the most talent and the most experience. But we didn't have the right team morale. Everybody got down and we struggled.

To be honest about it, my divorce messed up my head. I didn't want to put it that way to the press. But it played a big part in my season. Being away from my kids, especially.

Talking to my kids was a trouble for me. Most people don't understand that. I talked to my son. He's little but wise for his age. He'd tell me, well, Daddy, I want you to come home. I want you to come stay with me. Why do you have to stay in New York and I have to stay here in Los Angeles? That's hard to explain to a kid.

I had to go out there and play with that in my head. It's something you just have to bite down on. Everybody says they understand what you're going through, but few of them can really feel it the way you do.

After that last game, when the season's over for good, you sit there, and if you're not going on to the playoffs, you just think about how it went wrong. But I still tried to tell myself that we weren't 20 games out, that we were in the middle of it almost all season.

At this point in my career, I want to play baseball and be happy. I don't want to be frustrated because of what they write about me in the press all the time. Nobody can get the job done every year. The Mets have been winners, but the Mets can't win every year. And the Mets have made changes. In 1990, the team will be a different team.

I'm convinced that 1990 will be a better year for me. I should be healthy again, with all the injuries that bothered me behind me.

I have work to do on my head, too. I want my head to be clear next season. Going through a season and going through a divorce at the same time is tough on your mind. It's not Lisa who I miss. The most important thing to me is the kids. That's what got to me, being away from them. I was so accustomed to having them with me. When I came home from a road trip, the kids would be there, at home, in bed when I got home. It made me happy just to see them.

I've got to get that settled before next season. I want to come back and play ball again the way I know I can, with a clear head. Confident. I think it'll be a very important year for me.

I really look forward to it.

Who I Am

Who is Darryl Strawberry?

I like to think that I'm the kind of person people would think of as a very outspoken young man and at the same time a very friendly person. I'd like those who know me, and those who want to know me, to understand that I'm sincere, have a warm heart and am kind to people. I'll go out of my way to help people.

I hope that people won't think of me as someone who goes around saying nasty things. I don't do that.

I've always got something funny to say. I like to joke, to kid around. I think of myself as a likeable person. And I hope people realize that about me.

Of course, I get angry, too. Everybody gets angry about something. But I don't show it much; I keep a lot of it inside of me. Most of the time when I get angry, I don't say much about what's making me angry. But I may go out on the field and take it out on the baseball. When I'm mad, I go out on the field and whoever I'm facing that night, whoever the pitcher is, I'll take it out on him by hitting the ball as hard as I can. I think that's the best way to take frustration out.

I'm good at showing affection, too, to those I care about and those I love. I'm very good at showing affection because I'm a caring person. I'm not the type of guy who's caught up with what I'm doing. I'm caught up in life, in living, as a human being. I believe in learning, in getting better in every possible way. I believe in accepting others for what they are, not what they do or how much money they make.

I think of myself as a religious person. In some ways. I mention God's name from time to time. I don't go to church, because it's difficult, playing ball, finding time to do that. But as far as believing in the Lord, that's easy for me. I sit down and analyze my life, what happened to me when I was growing up as a kid, getting to where I am now, and I know that someone put me here.

I believe that the Lord put me here, in the position I'm in right now, because He felt that I was the perfect person to do what I do. It takes a lot to go through what I've been through and handle it as I have.

Sometimes I pray. Not as much as I should, to be truthful. But I do say my prayers at times and I thank the Lord. I let Him know that I am grateful for the blessings He's given me, the good things that He has provided for me.

In the playoffs against the Dodgers in '88, Orel Hershiser was thanking God, sort of meditating on the mound in gratitude. That didn't surprise me at all. You do thank the good Lord for all the good things that happen to you.

In sports, the guys who believe go through their careers in the limelight and they pray to God in different ways. They let the Lord know that they accept Him in their lives, they accept all the great things He made happen.

That's why I always ask the Lord to guide me in the right way. Guide me so that no one will ever think of me as a negative person. You give your prayers to God when he rewards you with something good.

I've learned a lot about myself over the years, since I was 18 and all this started for me.

I've learned not to abuse anyone you really love and care for. Don't take anything for granted about the people who are important to you. You have to realize that you're one of a different breed, something the Lord made you to be. He made you to cherish the people around you. He wanted you to realize how very important they are to you.

When I was just out of high school and into professional baseball, I probably did some bad things; you do a lot of bad things when you're young, things you know are wrong. But I tried not to hurt anybody.

You learn that you have to have a stable mind. You start to know what the things are that you want out of life. You discover the truth in your heart. And that's one rule that's very important to me: You've got to be true to yourself.

Thanks to the Lord, you can be anything and have everything you want because of where He put you. But I don't forget that the Lord put me here, and he didn't put me here to be something I'm not.

I don't believe in being silent, by the way. Yes, I sometimes hold back my anger. But I do believe that everybody, including me, is entitled to express just what he feels.

You don't have to destroy someone when you speak the truth to him, or to her. So don't keep it in. If you deliver the message that you have and get it out of your mind and out of your heart, it will make you feel more comfortable. When two people talk to each other, instead of being quiet, some thoughts go back and forth. It helps. It may not solve the biggest problems. I know that, for sure. But it's a good idea to talk.

Family is very important to me. I love my mother. I'm back in touch with my father. My brothers and sisters are very close to me, even if I'm a couple of thousand miles away a lot of the time. They can find me; I can find them. My kids matter to me more than almost anything I can think of. As I get older, I hope to start pushing everything aside for my family, especially the kids, spending more time with them. They're more important to me than all the other things I have to do.

I've been thinking about the baseball card shows that I do. You know, sign autographs, pick up some money, meet your fans. I've done quite a few, I guess. But I'm not sure that's a good way to use my time. Maybe I'd be better off going to a movie with a friend, taking the kids to an amusement park.

When you are as busy as I am as a ball player, you've got to keep an eye on your priorities. Some people have wanted me to get involved in politics, for instance. But I've never really considered myself to be a political person.

I hear a voice telling me to get up and go down there and vote. But I know that I don't really want to get up. I should do it, I suppose, but the majority of ball players I know, well, our minds are into something else. I don't pay much attention to what's happening in the news on television.

I'm aware of racism, of course. Who isn't? But I can honestly say that I've never been involved in a dispute or an angry scene that I thought was racial in nature. I played in the minors; all those towns were in the South. If I were going to discover racists, I would have found them down there. I'm not dumb. I've heard that they're down there, although probably not as openly as they once were. But I didn't find them.

I think the main reason is who I am. No white man is going to come up to me and start something. Of course, I'm not going to be in a place where I don't belong anyway, where I'm not comfortable. Even so, wherever I am, no one's going to come up and start saying racial things to me. Most of the people who want to see me, or meet me, look up to me.

But I'm not blind to racism. If I was someone nobody knew about, just some little black guy, a stranger, maybe it would be a totally different story. Then, it could become a very racial thing.

When I was a kid in south L.A., take my word for it, in my neighborhood there weren't any racial problems. Unusual, maybe, but true.

Sometimes I listen to Jesse Jackson and what he's saying makes sense to me. I haven't been the victim of racism, but I don't think he's too strong in his attacks on it. You can't be too strong about that. I think Jackson speaks for all blacks, to be honest about it, because the man is trying to deliver a message. It's about what's happened in the past and what is going on in the present. And everybody should be equal.

Human beings should behave as human beings, no matter what color they are. Black, white, yellow, Jew, Christian. We should all be human beings first and accept each other. The color of your skin doesn't affect the thoughts in your mind. There are maniacs out there who are white, who are black, who are yellow.

A few years ago there was a wonderful high school basketball player in Chicago. His name was Ben Wilson. He was one of the best college prospects in the country. I know what that's like. Well, Wilson got killed, over a gold chain that he had around his neck. Killed by another black kid. One black kid killing another. That's a tragedy.

When I read about things like that, I think that maybe there's something all black athletes ought to be doing to make life better for all those kids—the good, talented ones like Wilson and the angry ones, like the kid who shot him.

It would take a lot of time and a lot of courage. Get a bunch of well-known athletes together and go to high schools all over the country and just talk about life and pride and doing well in the real world, not the world of drugs and violence.

Say Michael Jordan and Magic Johnson and Doc Gooden and others, men like that, and I took the time to go into the schools, or just the streets. Let people know that we're out there for a good cause. Get the gangs together, one at a time, and sit there and deliver a message to them. Let them hear what comes from our hearts. We could tell them that there's always a way if you apply yourself to do something well. After all, they apply themselves to be gang members. And that's the road to death and to failure. Just think what might happen if they applied themselves to school, if they applied themselves in the classroom, learning how to read.

I go back to Crenshaw High School in L.A. I'm always back in my old neighborhood because that's where I work out in the off-season. You have to realize that no matter how high you get on that mountain, you're always going to be where you came from.

Being successful is great, but being yourself is great, too.

I never want to fool myself or fool anybody else. A lot of people do kid themselves into thinking that they don't have any roots. All they have is the house and the car and the piles of money they have *now*. Well, *then* is important, too, maybe more important.

I want to go out there and encourage those young kids. It's what Jesse Jackson has said about helping those kids to be somebody. You do have the opportunity in this life. There's nobody in the world who can sit and tell me that there's not a chance for everyone to go out there and be somebody. You can do it.

Going through what I grew up with, and coming through everything since, I know about that. After seeing the things I've seen, I know that how smart you are and how much smarter you can be is all in your own mind. What you want out of life is for you to decide.

You can do it by walking away from what's wrong and going on to what's right.

One of the frustrations is that you can't do it all by yourself. You've got to work with others. But in this country you can't always find people who want to work with you. Some of the big money-makers in business don't really care about the rest of the world. They don't want to take the time to make things better. They've got so much power and so much money that they don't want to stop making money to do some good. And you say to them, we've got to start taking time off for the ghetto people, to get rid of the drugs that are everywhere and to do good things for those in need. They look at you and say, "I've got too many things happening in my life."

They've got the power, but they don't have the time. You wonder why the world is turning into what it is? That's why. Somebody should shout, "Hey, you guys up there. The people are down here."

Somebody's got to take the time, because everywhere you look these days, there's someone in trouble. The homeless people have to sleep on the streets in winter because no one wants to take them in. The people with the power, the men in big business, with all their money going somewhere else, they just sit behind their desks and don't pay attention.

They want front-row seats for the World Series so everybody else can look at them and be in awe. But I know that they're not really very important. They don't do anything for our society.

They don't set an example. What can they teach a poor kid? Sure, they can teach him to get money above everything else. But that's it. You see them on television, going to their big dinners in their big bow ties. Charity events. They show up, smile, maybe give a few dollars and go back to their power games. There aren't many who give a lot of their lives to charity. Jerry Lewis does, and he's raised a lot of money for those kids. But he's rare.

I think of myself as a role model. And the good thing about it is that I never feel any pressure about it, because I know I'm a good person. All I have to do is be myself. I spend a lot of time with kids.

The press tells people that I'm this moody guy and that sort of stuff. It's not true. People have to understand that when you've been successful early in baseball, there's always going to be pressure in your life. You're never going to be able to please everybody. There'll always be someone who will feel that you could have done more than you did. One home run? Maybe two would have been better.

Being with kids may be the most important part of being a professional athlete. Seeing the kids, seeing how they care about you, is something that has to move you. They're not crazy about what you know or who you know or what everybody else thinks about you or what people say about you. They love you because of who you are and the way you go out there and play ball.

They are good judges of people.

It's not just my own kids that I love. I love all the kids. Maybe someday, I'll work with them. When I think about my life after baseball, if I continue to do well as a player and accomplish what I want to accomplish, I think about running a day-care center. I could spend time giving the kids a chance to have love from others, not only from their parents.

There is such a thing as good guidance. You can guide kids into the good ways of living. I'd like to be involved in that.

I guess I'll always be a fan of baseball, even after I finally retire. I will always enjoy the game, watching it, seeing the younger players come up. Maybe one day, I'll be sitting at home and watching my son on television playing ball, if that's what he chooses to do with his life.

I don't think I'd lean on him to be a baseball player. He's already so good at the age of four, it's hard to believe that this kid will not make it, but I won't apply pressure on him. Whatever he chooses to do, it'll be his choice.

Maybe by then, I'll have another occupation. You don't have to leave baseball and just sit around. I've had sports commentators tell me to think about getting into their business. They've told me that they think I'm articulate enough to comment on games and that I know what I'm talking about. And, of course, I speak my mind. I'd have to take some courses, but I wouldn't mind broadcasting.

By then, I hope I have a family together again. I learned something from the marriage and the kids and the divorce. I wouldn't want to be away from my family once I leave baseball.

I understand now how important it is to be with your wife and your kids. I want my kids to grow up and recognize their father not for what he gave them, but for making them appreciate what life is really all about.

And maybe when they're grown up, one of them can find out where the family name came from. I've never found out. I know I'm glad to be Darryl Strawberry instead of, say, Darryl Smith. It has a ring to it, Strawberry. People say to me, what a wonderful name. But I don't know the history of it. I never asked my father about it and I never met my grandfather; he wasn't around when we were growing up. Someday, I'm going to do a lot of research—or have one of the kids do it—and find out where Strawberry came from. It would be fun to know.

But first I've got to continue to play ball as well as I can.

In all honesty, I have to say that one objective is still ahead of me. That's getting into the baseball Hall of Fame. That's the ultimate achievement, for me and for every guy who ever played the game. I don't sit around thinking about it, however. That's somewhere way down the line. At this point in my career, still a young player, I go out and think, I'm the best player in the game. That's in my mind. I'm not being cocky about it. It's more a matter of confidence that comes from my heart. It's what I believe Darryl Strawberry can do each day on the field.

The more you believe in yourself, the more you can do. Every morning when I wake up and go to the ball park, as I prepare myself and put on the uniform, I tell myself, I am the best. I am determined to be the best.

Being Darryl Strawberry and having played in New York, where the pressure's always on, and overcoming all that, I'm now at a point where I'm relaxed. I believe that I can reach another level, a higher level, each year that I play ball.

I've gotten through the abuse from the press, dealing with their unrealistic expectations for me. I don't take abuse; I react to it. And I don't complain about it, either. Now, at last, that's behind me. I've found my own happiness and peace inside my heart. And it's bringing out the best in my ability on the field.

I know that there are threats out there. That's how it's always been. Drugs. Drink. Women. But if you're stable in your own mind and have that peace up there, you don't have to worry about it.

It starts with girls and ends with drugs.

That's happened to a lot of athletes. The girls like drugs and athletes. An athlete gets involved, and whenever he comes to town, there's the girl and the drugs. Next thing you know, you're hooked. You don't think you are. You leave town. But then you start seeing other people, maybe in the off-season. You get involved again. The kind of people you deal with, the kind of people that surround you, that's what makes you what you are.

You try to protect a teammate, if you think he's on the edge of trouble. Real trouble. Otherwise, it might just be his private business. You might say to a teammate, "Hey, man, stay away from that guy. He ain't no good."

You try to do whatever you can to prevent anything that's major from happening to a teammate you care about. Drugs can lead you into another world. They can change your whole personality, make you a different person. Your true friends should want to help you.

And if I'm going to do what I hope to do as a player between now and the last game of my career, I've got to know who I am and be proud of who I am.

I don't read everything that's written about me in the press. Sometimes, a friend lets me know about one article or another. Early in the '89 season, a friend told me to look at an article called "The Case for Darryl," in a New York publication called *7 Days*.

It was written by a guy I didn't think I'd met, named Rafael Yglesias. It was a flattering article about me and how, at times, I've been misunderstood or even underestimated. But part of it was about how children feel about me.

Yglesias wrote that children "watch the Straw's skyscraper shape, his scooping bat sculpt air and gape as the ball he hits repels gravity, escaping Shea's tense symmetry; Darryl himself waits at the plate, his left hand politely easing the bat to the ground, his Muppet face happily watching along with us, just as pleased. Kids love the impossible, the extravagant, the childish player because winning is still pure in them, not subverted by disappointment, envy, and weariness. They don't need to impress with the intelligence of their appreciation—they want the victory, the big event. They want Darryl."

That made me feel good.

Darryl: Epilogue

Maybe there ought to be a school for husbands. Maybe there ought to be a school for fathers. Certainly, when I look back on my life in and out of baseball in the last few years, I wonder if I was ready for everything that came my way.

I got married and I had to play a role I had never played before. I guess when I looked back on my parents' marriage, I didn't learn much. So I had to do the best I could do, without much knowledge or experience. I tried to be the best husband to Lisa that I could be, but she'd probably say that I didn't get a passing grade most of the time. I had to grow up in order to understand what she was telling me.

Then there were the children. I loved them from the moment they were born. I can't explain that; it's almost a religious thing inside of me. I looked at them and I loved them and I knew that I always would love them. Sure, I wasn't around as much as some fathers, guys with nine-to-five jobs. But even when I wasn't with them, I loved them. When I did spend time with them, I wanted them to know that and I think that they do know it.

So when Lisa and I weren't getting along, it was natural for me to fear that I'd lose my children. After all, if she left, they'd go with her, I thought. When that happened, my anger got to me and I turned it on her. The 1989 season was a bad one for me, as well, so everything seemed to combine to make my mood a sad and frustrated one.

That's why Lisa and I had that confrontation in California, the one that the press latched onto. It almost landed me in jail and that fact made me take a hard look at myself and what had been going on in my head. It wasn't easy for me to do that. I'd always had so much pride about my skills as a baseball player that it was hard for me to realize that I was less than a superstar as a family man.

Lisa and I had some good talks during all

that craziness in California during that off-season. I came to realize that I had a real problem with drinking. I know that I wasn't that kind of falling-down drunk that you see in bars. But I knew that I had developed a kind of dependence on the stuff, to keep me from having to deal with the problems of my life. It was time to repair the damage.

Thanks to the Mets and the team psychiatrist, I made my way back east to a clinic in Manhattan, for treatment. I spent a month in that clinic, paying attention to the lessons they were teaching me, living a clean life again, looking ahead to better times and to the achievements that mattered to me. I could look ahead, as well, to a better, peaceful life with Lisa and the children. That was important to me. So I did what I was told during that month in the clinic. When I got out, it was time for spring training again. That felt good. I headed down to Florida and got ready. The players' strike was on, of course, but I was able to work out on my own, as I'd always done, and when we got into the abbreviated spring training, I was ready.

It was going to be another season for me, one that I hoped would be far better than my dismal '89 season. I didn't want to look back on that; I'd thought about it enough. What was important now was for me to get back my old optimism about my talents and my objectives. To be in shape and to stay in shape. When the season began, I felt good. My relationship with Lisa had improved; I had access to my children again. That's what mattered most to me. So I could concentrate on the season itself. The Mets were a different team in '90, of course, with Frank Viola around all year and Doc back into his old groove. Of course, we were without Gary Carter and Keith Hernandez, among others, from the old days, but I hoped that they would find happier times, just as those of us who remained Mets would find them.

Above all, I knew that I had to take care of myself. You can't depend on anyone else taking care of you in this life. You've got to do it for yourself. So I set out to do just that. I didn't become one of those early-to-bed, early-to-rise fanatics; I didn't have to change my entire lifestyle. But I wanted to become more conscientious and pay closer attention to my own body and my own state of mind. If I could do that, I knew, I could be the player I always wanted to be, a player even better than the one who had done well during his first few years in the majors. At 28, I knew I had productive years, many of them, left in baseball. I had to remember that, to remind myself that my best years were ahead of me. I believed that.

It seems like so much has happened to me in just the few years I've been in professional baseball. I've told a lot of it in these pages, of course. But at this point in my life, I don't want to look back. I want to move ahead. And I'm convinced I can do that.

When you see me out there in right field, or at the plate, or when I'm running the bases, keep in mind that I've had my own trials off the field lately. And I've begun to deal with them. I know that I can't let up, that I can't forget that liquor has the power to destroy me. And I have the power to use it to destroy myself. It's not the booze that does you in; you do it to yourself.

I'm smarter now. I intend to prove that in every way, to Lisa, to the children and to my teammates. As long as I've got my pride, I know I can make my mark, on the field and off of it.

Darryl Strawberry

Career Statistics and Highlights
(From New York Mets Information Guide, 1989)

BIRTHDATE: March 12, 1962

BIRTHPLACE: Los Angeles, CA

BATS: L   THROWS: L

HEIGHT: 6-6   WEIGHT: 195

HOW OBTAINED: Mets' first selection (No. 1
pick in the nation overall) in the June
1980 Free Agent Draft.

SIGNED BY: Roger Jongewaard

CONTRACT STATUS: Option year, 1990

Team No. 18   Position: Right Field

1988—Became the Mets' all-time leading home run leader during the year... His seventh homer of the year, May 1 in Cincinnati against Pat Perry, gave him 154 for his career and tied him with Dave Kingman... Surpassed Kingman on May 3 when he cracked a three-run homer at Shea against Juan Eichelberger of the Braves.

Came in second in the voting for the National League Most Valuable Player Award ...Kirk Gibson won with 272 points while Darryl was second with 236 points... It was the highest point total by a Met since Tom Seaver had 243 points in 1969.

Led the National League with 39 home

runs ... The 39 homers tied his Mets' club record set in 1987 ... Was first in the League with a .545 slugging percentage, second in RBI with 101, tied for fourth with 101 runs scored, fourth with 296 total bases, fifth with 85 walks, tied for eighth with a .366 on base percentage, tied for fifth with 15 game-winning RBI, scored with 69 extra base hits, and third with 21 intentional walks.

Darryl and Kirk Gibson of the Dodgers are the only two players in the majors to hit 20 or more homers and steal 20 or more bases in each of the last five seasons.

Began the year with a flourish ... Cracked a solo homer in his first at bat of the year, April 4 in the second inning against the Expos' Dennis Martinez in Montreal ... It marked the third time in his career that he had homered in his first at-bat of the season ... Also accomplished the feat in 1987 and in 1984.

Hit another solo homer in the seventh inning aginst Randy St. Claire ... The ball hit the roof at Olympic Stadium and was measured to have gone 475 feet ... Had two singles and a walk in the game to go 4–4.

Celebrated his son Darryl Jr.'s third birthday on June 15 with his second multiple homer game of the year against the Cardinals at Shea ... Both of his homers, a two-run shot in the first, and a solo shot in the fourth, came against Chris Carpenter.

Named to start in the All-Star Game for the National League for the fifth year in a row ... Went 1–4 in the NL's 2–1 loss in Cincinnati on July 12.

Went 8–12 with five runs scored, three homers and four RBI in the season's first three games in Montreal ... His four RBI pushed him to 500 for his career.

Ran up a seven game hitting streak, from April 17–24 ... In the seven games, he went 12–25 (.480) ... Was hitting .397 (23–58) after 17 games on April 24 ... Put together five two-hit games in those seven contests.

Knocked in 11 runs in six games between April 30 and May 6 ... Had two hits and three RBI to pace an 8–0 victory over the Braves on May 3 for David Cone.

Cracked a dramatic two-out, two-run homer in the bottom of the 10th inning against John Franco, to lift the Mets to a 4–3 victory against Cincinnati, May 6 at Shea ... With two outs in the ninth, Keith Hernandez walked and then Strawberry belted his ninth homer ... Accounted for all four of the Mets' runs.

His average was .286 on May 17 ... Then went 11–26 (.423) to bring his average back to .309 on May 25 . . . Collected four hits in a 5–2 win in San Diego on May 18.

Had three hits, including a two-run first inning homer against Fernando Valenzuela, in a 5–2 win on May 22 in Los Angeles.

Ran up another solid stretch, June 4–21 . . . Hit safely in 13 of 15 games including an eight-game hitting streak from June 4–13 . . . Also in the 15 games, he had 6 homers and 17 RBI.

Came through with a two-run homer and a two-run single in a 6–2 triumph in St. Louis on June 6 . . . His two-run homer in the fifth inning on June 28 broke a 1–1 tie and propelled New York to its 5–2 win in Pittsburgh.

Came up with a big night in a 12–6 success against Houston at home on June 30 . . . Scored four runs, with three hits, including a triple, homer and two RBI.

Went 3–3 in a 3–2 victory against the Astros in the first game of a July 1st doubleheader at home.

Was hitting .284 at the All-Star Break . . . After the break he hit safely in seven straight (10–27, .370) with three homers and five RBI . . . Hit homers in three straight games, July 15–17 . . . Scored four runs for the second time on July 14 in Atlanta.

Collected three hits, three runs scored, with two doubles and a season-high five RBI in a 10–2 victory over the Phillies in Philadelphia on July 27.

Had three homers in consecutive games, September 18–21 . . . In those three games, he had six RBI, including two game-winners . . . From September 15 until the end of the year, he was 18–49 (.367) with six home runs and 13 RBI.

Belted his 30th homer against Craig Lefferts in San Francisco on August 16 . . . Only hit .191 with three homers and 12 RBI in August . . . His average fell to a season-low, .261 on September 2.

Picked up the pace again . . . Hit safely in six straight (September 3–9) with three homers and five RBI to bring his average back up to .266 on September 9.

On October 2, he had two homers against the Cardinals, his third multiple homer game of the year and his 18th of his career.

Voted to the Sporting News Silver Slugger Team and the Sporting News National League All-Star Team.

Batted .300 (9–30) with five runs scored, two doubles, a homer and six RBI in the seven League Championship Series Games vs. the Dodgers . . . Went 3–5 with three RBI to help pace the 8–4 victory in game three, October 8th in New York . . . Had a two-run homer in the third inning of game four in New York against John Tudor.

Has 160 home runs the last five years, second in the major leagues to Dale Murphy's 170.

Had the best home run percentage (9.62 per 100 at-bats) in the league against left-handed pitchers.

In the Majors (1983–1988)—In 1983, Darryl became the third Met to be selected the National League Rookie of the Year by the Baseball Writers Association of America... The other Mets to win the award were Tom Seaver in 1967 and Jon Matlack in 1972... Dwight Gooden became the fourth Met Rookie of the Year Award winner in 1984.

Received 18 of a possible 24 first-place votes and was the only rookie to be named on all 24 of the writers' ballots... Accumulated 106 points to 49 for second place finisher Craig McMurtry of the Atlanta Braves.

Also named the Sporting News National League Rookie Player of the Year.

Set the following Mets' club records:

—Most homers, left-handed batter (26); the old mark was 23 by John Milner in 1973.

—Most homers, rookie (26); the old record was 19 by Ron Swoboda in 1965.

—Most RBI, rookie (74); the old record was 65 by Steve Henderson in 1977.

With his 26 homers and 74 RBI, he led the National League rookies in those departments... Tied with Cincinnati's Gary Redus for the NL rookie lead in game-winning RBI with 11.

In the spring he was named the winner of the Johnny Murphy Award, emblematic of the top Mets' rookie in camp... Started off the year with Tidewater of the International League and was recalled by the Mets on May 4.

Made his major league debut in a 7–4, 13-inning triumph over the Reds at home on May 6... Went 0–4 with two walks and a stolen base... Wound up scoring the winning run when George Foster cracked a three-run homer.

Picked up his initial big league hit and RBI, a run-scoring single in the eighth inning against the Reds' Ben Hayes in a 10–5 triumph on May 8 in New York... Was 0–11 prior to the single.

On May 16, in his 27th big league at bat,

he belted his first major league homer, a two-run blast in the fifth inning against the Pirates' Lee Tunnell in Pittsburgh.

The next night, he hit his first Shea Stadium homer, a three-run shot against Tim Lollar of the Padres to provide the game-winning RBI in a 6–4 triumph.

After his first 24 games (through June 5) Darryl was hitting only .161 (14–87) with three homers and nine RBI...For the rest of the year (98 games), he would hit .282 (94–333) with 23 homers and 65 RBI.

In the first game of a two-night doubleheader in St. Louis on June 26, he rocked the Cardinals with two homers and his first five-RBI contest to ignite a 10–1 romp...Both homers came off Bob Forsch.

In 1984, Darryl led the Mets in RBI (97) and homers (26)...Finished fourth in the NL in homers, tied for fourth in RBI with the Cubs' Ron Cey and was eighth in the League in slugging percentage (.467).

Tied his then-Mets-club-record for homers in a season by a left-handed batter...With his 26 homers and 27 steals, he became only the second 20–20 man in Mets history...The first was Tommie Agee in 1970 (24 homers, 31 steals)...His 55 RBI after the All-Star break led the National League.

In his first 22 games, he batted .363 with five homers and 13 RBI... Homered off Mario Soto in his first at-bat of the season in the opener on April 2 at Cincinnati... It was the Mets' only run in the 8–1 loss.

Played center field for the first time in his major league career, April 4 at Cincinnati... Overall, he played 12 games in center, 10 starts.

Put together his first career four-hit game, in a 12–5 loss at Philadelphia on April 22... Had a three-run homer against Charles Hudson, three singles and four RBI... Ran his streak to 6–6 with a hit in his first at bat in a 6–4 loss at Montreal on April 23.

Tied a club record with three doubles (11th player to do it) in an 8–1 victory over the Cubs at home on May 1.

Collected his fifth career two-homer game on June 17 as the Mets lost to St. Louis, 6–3... Hit solo homer against Ricky Horton in the sixth inning, and in the eighth he hit his first career inside-the-park homer, against Bruce Sutter.

Was the starting right fielder for the NL in the All-Star Game in San Francisco on July 10, becoming the Mets' first All-Star starter since Dave Kingman in 1976... Went 1–2 in the NL's 3–1 win at Candlestick.

With 1,565,044 votes, he led all NL outfielders and was the third-best overall vote-getter in the League, trailing San Diego's Steve Garvey and Philadelphia's Mike Schmidt.

Stole three bases to tie a club record in a 9–6 loss at Cincinnati on July 19.

In 1985, he finished sixth in the National League with a career-high 29 home runs... Broke his own record for homers by a left-handed batter (26 in both 1983 and 1984)... Hit a then career-high .277... His .557 slugging average was the highest ever for a Met regular... Had an outstanding season statistically despite missing seven weeks with an injury to his right thumb that required surgery.

Had three multi-homer games... Fashioned two two-homer games and one three-homer game... Also had eight games with at least three RBI (two games with three RBI, four with four RBI, one with five RBI and one with seven RBI)... In addition, he had 30 multi-hit games (twenty-four games with two hits, four games with three hits and two games with four hits).

Voted an NL All-Star starter for the second straight year and was also honored twice as the League's Player of the Week.

Belted his first career grand slam (and first of two on the season) on April 28... It was a first-inning shot off the Pirates' Mike Bielecki in the Mets' 5–4, 18-inning victory at Shea.

In his 25th game of the season, Darryl suffered a tear of the inner ulnar collateral ligament of the right thumb when he made a diving catch of Juan Samuel's sinking liner in the third inning of the Mets' 4–0 win over the Phillies at Shea on May 11 . . . Two days later, surgery was performed to repair the ligaments . . . Dr. Richard Eaton performed the surgery, assisted by Mets team physician Dr. James Parkes . . . Darryl was placed on the disabled list the same day.

Darryl was hitting .215 with 6 homers and 12 RBI at the time of his injury . . . Was activated on June 28 and went 0–3 in that night's 3–2 loss at St. Louis . . . From the time of his activation through the end of the season, Darryl hit .297 (89–300) in 86 games, with 23 homers and 67 RBI.

Mets were 18–8 before Darryl was injured and went 20–23 during the period he was out . . . Team compiled a 60–33 record from his return through the end of the year.

Voted to start in the 1985 All-Star Game in Minnesota on July 16 . . . It was his second straight start, thus becoming the first Met ever to be voted to two straight All-Star

Games ... Was third among NL outfielders in the fan voting, behind Atlanta's Dale Murphy (1,425,952) and San Diego's Tony Gwynn (968,262) ... Darryl had 907,197 votes.

Was on base all three times up ... Singled, walked and was hit by a pitch ... Also scored two runs and stole a base in the NL's 6–1 win.

On July 20, he belted two homers (including his second grand slam of the season) and had a career-high seven RBI in the Mets' 16–4 win over the Braves at Shea ... His seven RBI were the most for a Met since Dave Kingman had a club record eight RBI against Los Angeles, June 4, 1976.

Darryl's biggest game during that season was his three-homer contest against the Cubs in the Mets' 7–2 win at Chicago on August 5 ... Joined Jim Hickman (1965), Dave Kingman (1976) and Claudell Washington (1980) as the other Mets who had hit three homers in a game (Gary Carter would join the group on September 3 in San Diego) ... Hit a three-run homer off Derek Botelho in the first inning, a solor homer off Botelho in the third and a solo drive to the center field bleachers off Ron Meridith in the seventh ... Also singled (for his second career four-hit game) and tied another club mark with 13 total bases ... Had five RBI on the day and scored four runs to tie an NL high for the year.

Collected one of the biggest hits of his career on October 1, a solor home run off Ken Dayley in the 11th inning in St. Louis that hit the right field digital clock, an estimated 440 feet from home plate...It provided the game's only run as the Mets defeated St. Louis, 1–0, in the first game of their crucial series.

In 1986, he tied with Atlanta's Bob Horner for sixth in the NL with 27 homers...Was second in slugging average (.507), seventh in RBI (93) and third in game-winning RBI (15).

Was the top vote collector in the majors for the July 15th All-Star Game in Houston...Had 1,619,511 votes...Became the first National Leaguer to be picked as an All-Star starter in each of his first three full seasons in the big leagues...Joe DiMaggio, Tony Oliva and Ron Carew were so honored in the American League...Went 1–2 in the game (a single against Milwaukee's Ted Higuera) in the American League's 3–2 win.

Came up with the first five-hit game of his career and the 17th in Mets' history in an 8–1 victory in Atlanta on April 30...Went 5–5 with a double and a two-run homer against Joe Johnson in the fifth inning...Scored two runs and knocked in three and raised his average from .254 to .313.

Fashioned the 10th multiple home run game of his career, collecting a pair against Mario Soto in a 7–2 win at Cincinnati on May 4.

Sparked a 6–5, 10-inning victory over Houston at Shea on July 3 . . . Hit two homers for his 11th multiple home run game of his career and his second of the year . . . Came up with four hits and four RBI.

Cracked his 100th career homer, a two-run shot against Ed Whitson . . . Became the third Met to reach that mark.

Garnered his 20th homer of the year, a solo against Bob Sebra, in the ninth inning of a 9–1 loss to Montreal at Shea on September 8 . . . It marked his fourth straight 20-homer season.

Belted his third career grand slam, a shot off Ray Krawczyk, in the fifth inning of the season finale, a 9–0 win over Pittsburgh on October . . . Also stole his 100th career base.

For the year, he had five four-RBI games and five three-RBI games . . . Had five two-steal games on the year.

Led all players in the League Championship Series against Houston with two homers and five RBI . . . Both of his homers brought the Mets back from behind . . . Three-run blast off Bob Knepper capped a four-run rally

in game three, tying the score 4–4 . . . Solo
shot off the right field foul screen against
Nolan Ryan tied up game five, 1–1 (Ryan had
retired the first 13 batters to face him up to
that point) . . . Doubled to start the decisive
three-run rally in the 16th inning of game
six, scoring the run that put the Mets ahead
to stay on Ray Knight's RBI single off Aurelio
Lopez.

Had two hits in game four of the World
Series as the Mets beat the Red Sox, 6–2 . . .
Belted a solo homer off Al Nipper in his final
series at bat, in the eighth inning of game
seven, to give the Mets breathing room in
their eventual 8–5 win.

In 1987, he became a member of baseball's
prestigious 30 homer–30 steal club, joining
Howard Johnson as the only pair of 30–30
teammates in baseball history.

Established Mets' club records for homers
(39), slugging average (.583), total bases
(310), extra base hits (76) and runs scored
(108) . . . Tied a club record with 97 walks . . .
With 104 RBI, he fell one shy of the Mets'
mark.

Finished third in the NL in homers, seventh in RBI, tenth in steals (36), third in
slugging average, ninth in on-base percentage (.398), seventh in runs scored and fourth

in walks ... His 151 hits and .284 batting average were a personal high.

Voted to start in the All-Star Game, becoming the first National Leaguer to be picked as an All-Star starter in each of his first four complete major league seasons ... Was sixth in voting for Most Valuable Player Award.

Got off to a flying start ... Hit safely in his first 10 games, his longest hitting streak of the season, with 1–36 (.361) ... Homered in each of the season's first three games, a first in Mets' history ... Had five homers and fifteen RBI in his first eight contests.

In his first at-bat of the season, he belted a three-run homer off Bob Patterson in the Mets' 3–2 Opening Day win against the Pirates, April 7 ... It marked the second time in his career that he'd homered on his first at-bat of the year (also in 1984 against Cincinnati's Mario Soto).

Collected his 500th major league hit on May 6, a single off Cincinnati's Ron Robinson in a 3–2 Mets victory ... Belted his 119th career homer (moving him past Ed Kranepool and into second place on the all-time Mets list) on May 22, a shot off Fernando Valenzuela in a 6–4 win over the Dodgers at Shea ... It was Darryl's first homer ever against Valenzuela.

Belted his first career pinch-hit homer on June 6, against the Pirates' Doug Drabek in a 4–2 Mets win at Shea...It was his first pinch-hit since August 5, 1984, as he'd gone 0–11 as a pinch-hitter since then.

Named to start the All-Star Game for the NL for the fourth year in a row...Garnered 1,255,651 votes, second among NL outfielders to the Reds' Eric Davis (1,810,391)... Went 0–2 in the NL's 13-inning 2–0 win at Oakland on July 14, 1987.

Moved into the cleanup spot in the order by Manager Davey Johnson, beginning on July 20...Was hitting .268 at the time of the move...Batted safely in 17 of his first 20 games in the fourth spot, with 24–69 (.345), 19 runs scored, 7 homers and 15 RBI...Average went from .268 to .283 on August 11 ...Included in this stretch was a nine-game hitting streak, July 21–31, with 12–35 (.343).

Overall on the seaon, he played 66 games in the cleanup spot, batting .303 (73–241), with 56 runs scored, 14 doubles, 18 homers and 52 RBI.

Had a big day in the Mets' 23–10 win at Chicago, August 16...Scored five runs to tie a club record (also held by Lenny Randle in 1978 and Lee Mazzilli in 1979)...Collected four hits and five RBI...Had two doubles, a triple and a homer, coming within a single of hitting for the cycle.

Banged his 30th homer of the year, breaking his own club mark for a left-handed hitter, off Mike Krukow in a 10–6, 10-inning loss to the Giants at Shea, August 19 ... Howard Johnson also hit his 30th homer in the game, giving the Mets two 30-homer hitters for the first time ever.

Was the NL Player of the Month for September ... In the month, he played in 27 games and hit .317 (33–104) with 24 runs scored, 9 doubles, 8 homers, 27 RBI and 11 steals.

Stole two bases in a 7–1 win at Chicago, September 21, to reach 30 steals and join Johnson in the 30–30 club ... Reached the 100-RBI mark for the first time with a sacrifice fly off Mike Bielecki in a 10–2 win over the Bucs at Shea, September 25.

In the minors—Singled to center in his first professional at bat for Kingsport in the Appalachian League in 1980 ... Hit 13 home runs and stole 31 bases for Lynchburg of the Carolina League in 1981.

In 1982, he was named the Most Valuable Player in the Texas League ... Led the league in home runs (34), walks (100) and slugging percentage (.604) ... His home run total was the most by a Texas League player since Chuck Harrison hit 40 in 1964 ... Was tied for second in the league in stolen bases (45) and third in the league in RBI (97) ... The 34 home runs were a Jackson franchise record (the old mark was 21 by Jody Davis in 1979).

Also established club marks for stolen bases (the old mark was 41 by Kelvin Dhapman in 1978), and his 93 runs scored topped the old Jackson standard of 91, which was held jointly by Lee Mazzilli and Mike Howard.

Named to the first team of Class AA All-Star Team . . . Promoted to Tidewater of the International League after Texas League playoffs . . . Appeared in five games and was 5–20 to help Tides capture International League Post-Season Championship . . . Had a homer, double and scored four runs.

Background—A graduate of Crenshaw High School, where he starred in basketball and baseball...Other graduates of Crenshaw include former NBA star Marques Johnson, former NFL halfback Wendell Tyler and Detroit Tigers infielder Chris Brown ...At Crenshaw, Darryl hit .371 with four home runs as a junior and .400 with five homers as a senior...Helped Crenshaw capture a city championship in basketball...Had numerous collegiate scholarship offers for basketball as well as baseball...A brother, Michael, played minor league ball with the Dodgers, while another brother, Ronnie, played collegiately in Los Angeles...Along

with Jeff Bittiger, he received the first an-
nual Doubleday Award, emblematic of the
Most Valuable Player on the Jackson team
in 1982.

YEAR	CLUB	AVG	G	AB	R	H	2B	3B	HR	RBI	BB	SO	SB
1980	Kingsport (Rookie)	.268	44	157	27	42	5	2	5	20	20	39	5
1981	Lynchburg (A)	.255	123	420	84	107	22	6	13	78	82	105	31
1982	Jackson (AA)	.283	129	435	93	123	19	9	34	97	100	145	45
1983	Tidewater (AAA)	.333	16	57	12	19	4	1	3	13	14	18	7
1983	Mets (NL)	.257	122	420	63	108	15	7	26	74	47	128	19
1984	Mets (NL)	.251	147	522	75	131	27	4	26	97	75	131	27
1985	Mets (NL)	.277	111	393	78	109	15	4	29	79	73	96	26
1986	Mets (NL)	.259	136	475	76	123	27	5	27	93	72	141	28
1987	Mets (NL)	.284	154	532	108	151	32	5	39	104	97	122	36
1988	Mets (NL)	.269	153	543	101	146	27	3	39	101	85	127	29
1989	Mets (NL)	.225	134	476	69	107	26	1	29	77	61	105	11